the little black book for girlz

the little black book for girlz

A Book on Healthy Sexuality

St. Stephen's Community House

annick press
toronto + new york + vancouver

This book contains general reference information about sexuality and health issues. It is not intended as a substitute for the advice of a trained medical professional. Readers should not attempt to diagnose or treat themselves based on material contained in this book, but rather should consult an appropriate medical professional before starting or stopping any medication and before implementing any other treatment discussed in this book. The authors and publisher are not responsible for any adverse effects resulting from the information contained in this book. The opinions expressed in this book are those of the contributors and do not reflect those of the publisher or St. Stephen's Community House. The contents of this book have been reviewed by a variety of health professionals to ensure medical accuracy.

© 2006 St. Stephen's Community House (text and illustrations)

Annick Press Ltd.
All rights reserved. No part of this work covered by the copyrights hereon may be reproduced or used in any form or by any means – graphic, electronic, or mechanical – without the prior written permission of the publisher.

We acknowledge the support of the Canada Council for the Arts, the Ontario Arts Council, and the Government of Canada through the Book Publishing Industry Development Program (BPIDP) for our publishing activities.

Cataloging in Publication

The little black book for girlz : a book on healthy sexuality / by St. Stephen's Community House.

Includes index.
ISBN-13: 978-1-55037-954-9 (pbk.)
ISBN-10: 1-55037-954-2 (pbk.)

1. Sex instruction for girls. 2. Teenage girls—Sexual behavior.
3. Teenage girls—Health and hygiene. I. St. Stephen's Community House (Toronto, Ont.)

HQ51.L58 2006   j613.9'55   C2006-901806-5

Distributed in Canada by:

Firefly Books Ltd.
66 Leek Crescent
Richmond Hill, ON
L4B 1H1

Published in the U.S.A. by Annick Press (U.S.) Ltd.

Distributed in the U.S.A. by:
Firefly Books (U.S.) Inc.
P.O. Box 1338
Ellicott Station
Buffalo, NY 14205

Printed and bound in Canada.

Visit us at: www.annickpress.com

Contents

Preface

No matter what age we are, many of us prefer to speak to our peers about experiences we are going through, especially around issues of sex and sexuality. Many young women have expressed to us that there is a lack of material they can relate to on sexuality and relationships. They want something not only aimed at them, but also created by them. Out of this frustration came *The Little Black Book for Girlz*. The book was created by young women who hung out at the St. Stephen's Community House Youth Arcade Drop-In, in downtown Toronto. As a group we had many discussions about all kinds of different issues. These discussions were very honest and non-judgmental, and the girls wanted sex ed. material that was equally positive and empowering to them. As a group we decided to write our own book that would encourage other young women to learn more about their bodies, their relationship, and their lives.

The Youth Arcade was an ideal environment for this project. It is a space where youth can meet, share experiences, identify problems, and support each other. It is also a place where they are challenged to think critically about the world around them. By having this space, the girls were able to take responsibility for the creation of the book and able to honestly talk and write about their lives.

At the time, and in such a supportive atmosphere, we felt very brave and powerful. We thought, "A book? No problem!" Well it turned out to be a little harder than we expected. Sex and relationships are HUGE subjects. To keep the book a manageable size, we had to cut out entire chapters on issues like body image, childhood sexual abuse, media, and religion. At times many of the writers were frustrated by the process and had other issues they were dealing with at home and school. It took two years and constant revisions with a number of youth and community professionals, including social workers and doctors, to edit and review it … and here we are today.

We're happy to report that the young women involved with *The Little Black Book* have become local superstars for their work on the project. Their names have popped up on television, on radio, and in magazines, all praising the girls for their honesty, their edge, and their creative spirit.

At St. Stephen's Community House we feel that material directed at youth is most effective when written by youth. Our hope is that this book offers information without judgment—without making girls feel bad about who they are and the decisions they make. We want our readers to feel intrigued, better educated, more capable of looking after themselves, and generally better able to make safe and fulfilling decisions regarding sex and relationships. To help in all this, we have included a resource guide and a glossary at the back of the book. Reading about all these issues may bring up questions that are not answered in *The Little Black Book*, so please check out the websites and hotlines that are listed if you require additional information. We hope you enjoy the book.

Sincerely,
Bridget Sinclair, *Project Coordinator and Facilitator*
Marlon Merraro, *Manager, Youth Services*
St. Stephen's Community House

hum dee dee dum dum dum...

Introduction

Alright, you chiquitas.
Welcome to
THE LITTLE BLACK BOOK.

In your very two hands, you hold a copy of a publication created especially for and by young women. It's a special book all about healthy sexuality and we're super proud of it. Why? Because this book was put together by a diverse group of teenage girls who have questions (and sometimes answers) about what and why and who we are as young women.

This book is just full of great stuff. Inside you'll find stories of personal experiences, poetry, important information, and resources all written and put together by young women aged 14 to 18. We look at relationships, periods, sex, birth control, pregnancy, STIs and AIDs, abortion, and sexual assault. Most of the authors of this book gained a lot of their knowledge from being "Arcade kids" (hanging out at the youth drop-in program at St. Stephen's Community House). And we interviewed many experts around Toronto to get straight facts about the stuff we chiquitas have to deal with.

I think young women in Toronto are among the luckiest creatures on this planet. We live in an amazing city, in a culture that allows us to be who and what we want. It can be hard to know what to

do with these freedoms, and it's a drag dealing with any limitations. Many times we aren't given the respect that we deserve. Sometimes we are asked to be silent.

We of THE LITTLE BLACK BOOK FOR GIRLZ group realize that all women everywhere deserve a voice. This collective of girls understands the importance of voicing our opinions and sharing experiences and stories. Adults can tell us what they think we're dealing with, but can they KNOW? We felt it was important for young women to have a book dedicated to what we think matters. Wherever you are in your life, there's one fundamental thing that links us all:

We are teenage girls and we kick ass!

So please read on. Enjoy. Ask. Question. Talk to your friends, families, and lovers. It is super important to understand who and what you are and where you can go. And if you're ever stuck, please feel free to contact us or any of the organizations listed at the back of this book.

Signing off,
Chi Nguyen

THE AUTHORS

Corrine Aberdeen

Hello my name is … Corrine Aberdeen. This is an amazing book that I'm so happy to have been a part of. This experience ranks up there with being born and graduating from high school. The fact that you are reading this little book is pretty cool and the fact that I was able to contribute is even cooler. I really hope that all the information you learn from this book is useful to you, your friends, and even possibly family for many years to come. Ciao!!!

Emma Brown

My name is Emma Brown and I go to art school. My favorite artists are John Scott and Cindy Sherman. I live in downtown Toronto and I am 16 years old. I know some people will object to the content of this book, but the issues discussed here are what's going on for young women. They need to be talked about. These problems are not going to go away on their own.

I like dogs, especially my dog Georgia. I cannot wait to get out of high school. When I leave I will start my own radio show and give advice on relationships. I'm into riot grrl music like Babes in Toyland, L7, 7 Year Bitch, and Bikini Kill. I like to read fashion mags and independent zines. A really cool zine is *There Once Was a Train*. I hope you enjoy this book as much as I have.

Imogen Birchard

Oookie...my name's Imogen Birchard and I don't really know how to write these things so bear with me! I'm 17 years old and I've always lived in downtown Toronto, one of the best places in the world. I heard about *The Little Black Book* project for the first time when I was in grade 8. I thought it was rockin' then, and I'm glad to be a part of it now. I hope this book helps y'all like it helped me, and that you have fun reading it (cuz I know I had fun writing it). Enjoy!

Annie Grainger

My name is Annie Grainger. I got involved in writing this book through my time spent at the Drug-Free Arcade and working on the Venus Girls project. I became interested in *The Little Black Book* through my interests in female sexuality, young women's lives, growth, and well-being.

I've spent the last couple of years exploring my own sexuality. From the point of view of where I am now, I wanted to share some of what I have discovered and learned.

I live in Toronto and look forward to being finished high school so I can be free to live as I want to. I want to travel and explore the cultures, values, spirituality, and history of other countries. I hope you learn as much from this book as I have.

Rebecca Hodgson-Dewitt

My name is Rebecca Hodgson-Dewitt. I'm 19. I got involved with *The Little Black Book* because these issues are important to me and I feel they affect every young woman out there. I wanted to share some of my experience and knowledge with other young women in hopes that they will find it easier finding out who they are. I got connected to this project through hanging out at the Arcade. It's taken me several years to figure out what was good for me and I often learned the hard way. I dropped out of school in grade 10 but I found alternative educational programs, which I think gives you way more hands-on, life experience. What I hope you get out of reading this book is a better sense of who you are, more security in yourself, and the freedom to choose what and who you want to be.

Chi Nguyen

La la la … *moi, je m'appelle* Chi Nguyen. So, I grew up in Toronto and that means that I am a lucky chiquita. And, I'm even luckier to have been a part of *The Little Black Book*. This book represents a whole lotta wunderbar things— one being that we as young women have something to say, and that we got our shit together to say it.

The pursuit of "higher education" has taken me away temporarily from my city of youth. I have recently left to study at McGill in Montreal. It's cool. I'll be back. I dream of strong men and stronger women who care about each other and who never stop doing what makes them happy. I dream of blue skies, smiling faces, pretty sunsets, and perfect moments worthy of 8mm film. I love my girls and my kids. You should love yours too.

Kristina Pelletier

My name is Kristina Pelletier. This book has given me the opportunity to write something that will be read by lots of other people. I also got to spend a long period of time working with a wonderful bunch of girls.

Opportunities like this don't just pop up in front of your face: you have to go out into the world and discover them for yourself. I really wish that every-

13

one got a chance to accomplish something so unique and special as we did.

I am the sign of the Scorpio, therefore I can be a sweet little angel or a nasty rotten devil. My friends would describe me as two things, quiet but also completely hilarious. I'm kinda a two-in-one combination. If you know what I'm sayin'.

Hilary Quigley

Hi, my name is Hilary Quigley. I live in Toronto. I heard of this project through St. Stephen's Drug-Free Arcade, where I help write for the Venus Girls Project. I was really happy to get to work on *The Little Black Book*. I've learned a lot and had a stressful yet very enjoyable time. In the rest of my life I am relaxed. I'm learning how to fix the underside of the car world. Car mechanics that is. I like wire and pliers and making metal jewelry. I'm becoming a rich millionaire because of my crafty expertise. I am also a pro-talented screamer. *The Little Black Book* has helped me become informed in a way that I wouldn't have been without it. Violence sucks. And I hope this book doesn't become tacky with age, like all the eighties things.

Suvi Siu

My name is Suvi Siu. The most valuable thing to me, other than my loved ones, is my knowledge … it's priceless and it's something no one can ever take away from me. I may not have the highest IQ (which is what most people consider knowledge), but I do have a unique perspective on life. I'm one of a kind. I see things the way nobody else does. My thoughts, feelings, and ideas never stop flowing. I always have something to say, and I never leave a scene unnoticed. I reach for the stars, although I know I'll never get to touch them. I hope this book inspires you and that you learn as much as I have. Enjoy.

Chauntae Walls

My name is Chauntae Walls. I was sitting in class one day and my teacher showed me the information about *The Little Black Book*. I am really interested in writing so I thought this would be a good experience for me.

I've had my own experience of the struggles we face as young girls, and I wanted to write this book to try to help other girls understand what's really going on out there.

I live in Toronto, and I'm currently working part-time and will be enrolling myself back into school soon. My favorite subject is English and I plan on writing a book on my own someday. I hope within this book you will find answers to some of your questions.

Relationships

Chapter 1

In this chapter, we look at issues around entering into relationships and that whole crazy love thing. Why are relationships so important to girls? Well, obviously the way in which we interact with the rest of the world effects how we view ourselves. Whether it's a relationship with a friend, a lover, or a boy- or girlfriend, they can often be fun, exciting, and totally terrifying at the same time. Sigh ...

—Chi Nguyen

Suvi Siu

By night U were my friend

At the time
That meant more to U than it did to me.
I was too blind to see that U wanted more from me
I told U how deep I had fallen in love.
And when he started to creep U were the one
That showed me love. Why didn't I see
Yours I was suppose to be?

So because of us U were joyous.
I saw the glow in your eyes. And the happiness in your smiles
But U told me lies.
U made me feel the way I always felt in my dreams
My dreams came true in U
And U said U felt the same way too.
Then Y did you leave me
The way U did
U say things have changed. But it's not me
It's U that's changed
So strange

U say U never look in anyone's eyes
But all U tell is lies. U know what I have been through
Can U hear my silent cries. Look what U are doing to me
I open my eyes and now I see. Just when I finally trusted U
U turn around and lie to me too.
I am sorry I met U
U keep pushing me away. All I want is for U to be okay
But maybe U are right. I'll try not to fight
Since U are happy the way things are
I won't interfere. If that's the only way I can show I care.
But this is so tough

And it even gets more rough. Cause it's breaking my heart
Thinking I have done something wrong.
Maybe you planned this all along
To think U were so special to me, but now I see.
This is how it's going to be.
But it's my bad
"Ain't that sad"
"Cause I always see people the way I like to see them
From near or far and not for who they really are"
If this is love then it's not enough
If all I am is confused
Love would stay with me until the end and much longer
Why can't U at least be my friend?

Alicia Michele B.

What Is Love?

This warm and fuzzy feeling…my god that sounds clichéd. It's so overwhelming sometimes! It will literally take your breath away, you just can't believe that this happening to you. When I'm with him, I feel perfect. I feel like I am flawless. Wow, it's corny, ain't it? But I'm trying my best. Love…lovelovelove, the word crawls up from your gut into your windpipe when you're around that one person and just sits there, making it hard to say anything but

I Love You

Even just to clear your throat.

In French they say *amour*, in German *Liebe*, in Italian *amore*, in any language they all boil down to the same thing: LOVE.
But what exactly is love?
According to dictionaries and encyclopedias love is…
1. To feel tender affection for somebody
2. To feel desire physically and emotionally for somebody
3. To like something very much
4. To show kindness to somebody
5. To have sex with somebody
But surely some can apply without the others! Love is a complex thing to understand, let alone define but one thing is certain, whether in France, Germany, or Italy, love is love.

Imogen Birchard

Emma Brown

18

What Is a Healthy Relationship?

Rebecca Hodgson-Dewitt

* Feeling safe and able to talk about things that are important to you

* Feeling trusted and trusting your boy/girlfriend

* H A V I N G   F U N

* Feeling supported by your boy/girlfriend

* Not feeling pressured to do anything you don't want to do

* The relationship should make you feel good about yourself

* Able to decide when you are ready to have sex

* Learning about yourself and growing with each other

Reading the Signs: Unhealthy Relationships

- Mind games
- Controlling (telling partner what to do, etc.)
- Demanding (demanding sexual favors, etc.)
- Judgmental
- Smothering
- Pushing, hitting
- Grabbing, throwing objects
- Extreme jealousy
- Co-dependant (partner feeling like they can't do anything without you, vice versa)
- Public humiliation of partner
- Threatening
- Manipulation (tricking you into things you don't want to do, etc.)
- Possessive (treating your partner like they belong to you, are your possession, etc.)
- Overly critical
- Rough (pushing you around, being rougher during sex than you like, etc.)

—Imogen Birchard

Cheating: What is it?

Flirting? Having an emotional bond? Kissing? Talking? Sex...?

There are lots of different ideas of what cheating is. Some people think that flirting with someone else is cheating, while others think that as long as their partner isn't sleeping with anyone else, it's all good. When you're getting into a serious relationship, talk to your partner about what they think cheating is, and find a definition that you are both comfortable with to prevent any misunderstanding. Trust me, you'll avoid a lot of hurt feelings.   Imogen Birchard

Relationship Fundamentals

Mutual Respect: Sally is really in the mood and is ready to hit the sack with Alice, but Alice doesn't really feel like it. Alice feels comfortable telling Sally, "Not tonight, babe" and Sally respects Alice's boundaries and decisions.

Equality: Julie gives Pat a blow job, and after he comes, he goes down on Julie. They believe that they should have equality and reciprocity in their relationship ... especially in the bedroom!

Trust: Richard is talking to his old friend Suzie on the sidewalk when his girlfriend, Theresa, walks by. She doesn't go ape-shit on Richard or accuse him of cheating. She trusts Richard.

Honesty: When Dorah's ex-boyfriend calls her up for coffee, she decides that she's ready to let the past be the past and be friends. She mentions it to her boyfriend, Mark, because she wants him to know that she is totally honest with him about her decisions, even ones involving ex-boyfriends.

Separate Identities: Todd and Meridith care for each other very much, but they know who they are and don't want to meld into one! They have separate friends and activities, and their lives don't revolve around each other. They believe it's important to maintain separate identities.

Support: Greg's had a really rough day and needs a shoulder to cry on. Even though Abbie isn't used to men showing their emotions, she understands that Greg is someone she cares about and therefore wants to help and support him when he needs it.

Communication: Nick and Karen COMMUNICATE ... hurrah for them! They talk to each other about things they feel are important, like their feelings, sex, and hopes and dreams. Isn't that sweet? Seriously, it's important.

Imogen Birchard

LIES

I tell myself not to believe such a thing could happen to me but deep down inside, I know it's true. I ask myself why me, why me? Why would he do such a thing to me? To someone so honest and so true, I knew it all couldn't be true! It was all too real!

We started out as boyfriend and girlfriend. Things seemed fine, so amazing. I couldn't believe I was in such a deep relationship, together, part of a team. We had been together for four months, going on five. I thought it was the most romantic relationship anyone had ever been in. It felt so real. It just had to last forever. Most teen relationships are just not a "forever thing" but in a huge way I knew this one could be. It was the kind of real-life thing, not some shitty little kid's stuff that only lasts a month max!

As time went by it was just getting better and better. We were tight, closer than close. My friends had never seen a relationship like this before and neither had I. Seven months went by. I knew he was the one for me, even though we hadn't had sex yet. I dreamed that someday we would have a child and still be in love!

As July slowly came around the corner I found out something embarrassing and horrible that killed me deep down inside. This supposedly wonderful relationship came to an end; my "dream lover" had been cheating on me for seven months! One of his friends ratted him out by telling me every detail. I was crushed and ashamed!

I wanted to know more, more from him! So I decided to ask him about everything. What made me feel even worse inside was the way he answered me when I asked him about the affair, he said "It just happened!" How could something like this just happen? Why would a human being do this to someone and kill them inside? Kill their courage? How can I ever trust anyone again?

I was dead for a long time. In a way I was glad that this situation happened to me. I went on slowly and surely. I went on. I survived.

Kristina Pelletier

True friends

A true friend listens to what you say
Life is a sculpture, friends are clay
Friends are notes to life's great songs
A melody that carries you along
Whether it's joy or fear, they are here
In a world of darkness, friends are light
So thank your lucky stars tonight
When life gets hard and goals seem far
It's then when you know who
Your true friends are.

Alexander Tobar

When in Heaven

One day when the time is right
I'll come looking for you
And you can tell me if everything
I've heard is true

You can meet me in your
Favorite spot
We'll talk, I'll cry, I'll sing
You'll teach me how to fly on our
Silver-coated wings

I know we are different in every way
But minds we seem to share
The sudden feelings of empathy
And the eternal crosses we bear

They knew the end was close for you
But they never guessed for me
Once my confusion started
Living, I could never be

The things I never wanted
Now are left behind
The cold hard memories that hurt so much
For his emotion were stubbornly blind

Fox F.

girls with boys

girls with girls

Out, Gay, and Seventeen

Interview by Annie Gainger with an anonymous youth

Q. When did you know you were gay?

A. Well, I guess deep down I always knew since I was a kid and playing doctor with my girlfriends. But in grade eight I started to go out more and explore Toronto and meet people. Quickly I learned about this thing called "the lesbian community". I was intrigued. I didn't officially come out to myself until a year ago. But I always knew.

Q. What is different about your life compared to a heterosexual person's?

A. A lot is different and a lot is the same. I fall in love with girls, not boys. I want to live in a community where I am supported and where there are other girls who have similar lives so I don't feel isolated. There are many differences in terms of the oppression I will have to deal with and media images of gay youth and ... I could go on and on; I guess the main thing is I fall in love with girls.

Q. Does your family know?

A. Yes, they do now. I think my mom wasn't surprised but my dad and sister were. They are great though: supportive and understanding. I guess they were worried I would really change and be a different person but quickly they realized that was not the case. I am rare. Most of my friends who are gay have not told their parents for fear of being rejected or kicked out. I am really, really lucky. I got my mom involved in PFLAG (Parents, Families and Friends of Lesbians and Gays—see resource guide) and they helped my parents to deal with it all and provided them with a ton of support.

Q. What did your friends say?

A. I lost a lot of them. I changed schools. I told my two best friends and I thought they would be cool and, well, I was wrong. They told half the school and I was harassed by a number of guys until I left the school. I learned a lot about trust and what real friendship means. It was horrible actually, and I didn't really get a lot of support from my friends. But, hey, my family was great and now I am in a better place. Teachers should all have to have anti-homophobia training.

Q. Why do you think some people have such a hard time with gay people?

A. I think we are all influenced by parents, TV, and schools. A lot of adults are homophobic and teach it to their kids. Girls seem to get freaked out by gay girls because they worry that the gay girls will come on to them or that they may also be gay. I think some guys are freaked out because gay girls make them feel they don't have power in the way they expect or because it feels like a rejection. There is that thing of it being OK for girls to be gay if guys can watch. Well, that's mostly about immaturity. I think it's all about fear and ignorance. It's really sad actually, because they only limit themselves.

Q. How can straight youth be more supportive towards gay youth?

A. Well, it's hard because it should start with their parents, the school system, the media and so on. People can learn and be open minded, to step outside of themselves and not be so self-involved. They also have to realize that just 'cause their friend is gay they are still the same person. So many people think if you are gay, you want to sleep with everyone. Well, that's not the case! Educate yourself and grow up!

Q. What are some words of advice for other queer youth?

A. I guess make sure you can trust the people you tell. Get involved in a group for queer youth then you will know for sure you have people who will understand what you are going through. And have fun! Coming out is not the end of the world!

Being bisexual for me just means that I have the freedom to fall in love with another human being. Whether it be a male or female.

I am 18 years old and bisexual.

For the past year I had been wondering if I was bisexual. One day it became clear to me. I realized that I had fallen in love with another woman.

I had spent my whole life being attracted to men. And I thought that was the only way for me.

It was hard for me to realize my feelings towards other women when I still felt attracted to men. But I knew what I felt in my heart. And my heart does not lie. Anyway, I know from experience that it is still not easy being a teenager and being bisexual or gay. **The fear of not being accepted by your friends or family and society itself can be really scary.** But knowing when you are truly happy can help calm your fears.

I was always questioning myself and I was scared and wanted to deny any feelings I had for women. Even though I knew that being gay, lesbian, or bisexual was completely normal, it was still hard for me. I think for me the hardest thing yet is still getting up enough courage to tell my mom. Maybe one day I will have the courage to tell her and have her meet my girlfriend.

Anonymous, 18

Maddy Junipalier

WHAT'S ALL THE FUSS ABOUT?

Okay, I know it may seem different to you when you see two people of the same sex walking down the street holding hands or kissing on a park bench. But by now, especially if you live in downtown Toronto, you should be used to it. When two people of the same sex are together, they don't harm anyone—so why do some people hate gay and lesbian people?

Most children are not taught at home that it's okay to see or be a lesbian or a gay person. When some children see gay and lesbian stuff on TV or out in the public, they freak out and make nasty comments or laugh. It's just not right. Why does it matter so much when two people of the same sex like each other?

I know there are some people who don't like seeing it, but, hey, if you don't like it, turn your head. Haven't your parents ever taught you that if you don't have anything nice to say, don't say anything at all?

When you see a gay or lesbian person, what do you see?

Do you see a person with three rabbit ears and two ram's horns and a cat tail, two elephant tusks, and six dog paws? Or do you see a "normal" regular looking human being? With two ears just like you, two eyes just like your mom, two legs just like your best friend, and two arms just like your sister. **If so, then**

what are you staring at?

Gay and lesbian people are human beings. They are living, breathing people. They are cousins, dentists, lawyers, brothers and sisters, taxi and streetcar drivers. So what is all the fuss about?

Masculine

Feminine

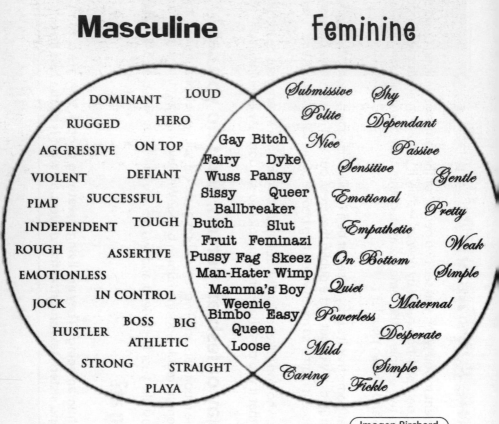

Masculine
DOMINANT LOUD
RUGGED HERO
AGGRESSIVE ON TOP
VIOLENT DEFIANT
PIMP SUCCESSFUL
INDEPENDENT TOUGH
ROUGH ASSERTIVE
EMOTIONLESS
JOCK IN CONTROL
BOSS BIG
HUSTLER
ATHLETIC
STRONG STRAIGHT
PLAYA

Overlap
Gay Bitch
Fairy Dyke
Wuss Pansy
Sissy Queer
Ballbreaker
Butch Slut
Fruit Feminazi
Pussy Fag Skeez
Man-Hater Wimp
Mamma's Boy
Weenie
Bimbo Easy
Queen
Loose

Feminine
Submissive Shy
Polite Dependant
Nice Passive
Sensitive Gentle
Emotional Pretty
Empathetic Weak
On Bottom Simple
Quiet Maternal
Powerless Desperate
Mild Simple
Caring Fickle

Imogen Birchard

These stereotypes of men and women create unhealthy and unsafe environments for everyone, especially women. By portraying men as dominant and women as submissive, women are forced to stay in their subordinate status in society.

Emotional, physical, and verbal abuse is nurtured in a society where men are entitled and strong, and women are quiet and weak.

ONCE A GIRL, NOW A BOY

Interview with Cat on Being Transgendered

Interview by Nirupa Varatharasan and Michelle Soltau, Additional information and research by Corrine Aberdeen

We had the absolute pleasure of interviewing Cat. We had called the 519 Community Center in the gay village and asked if anyone does workshops on trangender issues. Cat was kind enough to come in and do a workshop with us on everything from understnding terminology to what it was like for him to go through the process of identifying as female to identifiyng as male. We had A LOT of questions and there were A LOT of things we didn't understand – but Cat helped make things a lot more clear.

Transgendered: A broad term that describes people who transgress society's ideas of biological sex and gender norms and begin a self motivated transformation to have a lived identity as another gender (meaning people who are identified at birth as being a girl but live and walk through the world as a boy, or vice versa).

Gender: The social construct that masculinity and femininity are attributable to male and female physical bodies

Sex: The biological physical body, its reproductive organs, its secondary sex characteristics; male and female as defined by doctors at birth.

Transgendered people feel that the gender they appear to be physically does not match the gender they feel they are inside (i.e., a boy in a girl's body or vice versa). Imagine not being able to be yourself and having to constantly deny how you feel, what you believe, and who you are; these are some of the issues that young transgendered people struggle with from day to day.

Most transgendered people are aware of these feelings from as early on in life as childhood. In many cases when children begin to show their displeasure with their gender, they are diagnosed with gender dysphoria (clinical term for unhappiness with one's gender). Not every transgendered person is gay/lesbian; in fact being transgendered has nothing to do with sexual preference.

Support groups are available worldwide and are only a quick on-line search away. These groups help transgendered people explore the choices available such as living "in role" as a person of the sex they feel they are or gender-reassignment (sex change) surgery or hormonal treatments. Many issues take place in the lives of transgendered people, including coming out, acceptance from themselves and their family and friends.

N&M: Where are you in the process of transitioning?
C: Well, I've been through the Clarke Institute, which is a mental health facility in Toronto, and I have spoken with the psychiatrist, family doctor, and my family. I've had upper body surgery to remove my breasts, and I inject testosterone on a daily basis.

N&M: What made you change your sex?
C: I didn't actually feel like a girl or a guy; I felt like a person stuck in between. This year I went to a conference and that made me decide. In this world you cannot be in between, and therefore since I felt more like a guy than a girl, I changed my appearance.

N&M: How do you identify?
C: As a sissy boy! I don't act like a typical guy. I like to call myself a homemade guy because of the marks from the surgery I went through.

N&M: How does it feel to be a transgendered person?
C: It's a difficult process to go through. Everything about you is so different from other people and it is hard to understand how you feel. I have lost some friends, although there has always been support.

N&M: How much does the surgery cost?
C: In Canada upper body surgery for female-to-male costs anywhere from $5 000 to $10 000. Bottom surgery for female-to-males costs anywhere from $60 000 to $100 000, for male-to-female is $10 000 to $20 000. So yeah, pretty expensive! I'm not sure how much it costs in the United States. (See the resources section for how to find more info.)

N&M: How do you handle starting new relationships and telling them about transitioning?
C: Being very open from the start really helps. Seeing their reactions is rather amusing. You usually know how the person feels about you when you tell them. You find out if they like your personality or your gender!

N&M: When having sex, do you consider yourself straight?
C: No, I consider myself gay, not straight. It's playing with gender roles. I don't know, I date girls.

N&M: Have you experienced any problems with your vital organs after surgery?
C: No, although you can get uterine cancer, when your ovaries shrink. I have not experienced any problems with my organs, as of yet.

N&M: Who experiences more prejudices, M-to-F's or F-to-M's?
C: I think male-to-females experience more prejudice than female-to-males because they need to conceal more facial hair, and society has very strict ideas about men.

My skin's turned to driftwood tonight

My skin's turned to driftwood tonight
And everything that burns
And everything that floats

I'm mid-air, a mirror boat
Music all over the walls of your room
Snatch me there, boy
Unhook me onto you
I'll find my wet way over every quiet place
While you hold the world behind my back

Then, under all this black
And your laugh that's part surprise
I squeeze my knee between your wooden thighs
Gather my used goods about me like this blanket
to the floor
So, Sleep
You could press your fist through me now
I'm only air

Lea Weir, 19

To Jane, If You Care What I Was Thinking

Lea Weir, 19

You laughed, your tongue shining and your head in the sky. As usual you had me on my knees, but this time I was in the gravel and there were ruts and pits deep in my little-girl skin for hours afterward. You knew even then that I loved you. Your grimy child hands and dirty fingernails held the apple you didn't know I'd stolen from your kitchen just out of reach, and when I tried to struggle to my feet those same hands pushed me down. I could have gotten up. I was bigger than you were then. And I looked up your nostrils to the sweet pink tops, wanted to touch you there, before you turned and threw my apple. As far as you could.

Everything about you still shines as you walk down this city street, laughing into the wind and cement. Those wide black eyes still watch something over my shoulder as I talk to you.

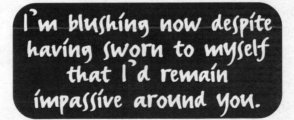

I'm blushing now despite having sworn to myself that I'd remain impassive around you.

Can't even believe it's really you; "Jesus, how long's it been?"

Twenty years. And too many dreams to count were of your lips and fingers, and sometimes, still, when I write, it's of you.

We're standing near a coffee shop so you invite me for a drink. We sit down in a deeply wooden corner and I stare as you unconsciously primp and preen under my scrutiny, straightening this, adjusting that, while quickly flinging your life across the table. The husband you loved, his lover you hate, the divorce. Ugly, oh so ugly, all of it. You make a face. Those boys, you can hardly remember what they looked like. That one girl. I'm blushing now despite having sworn to myself that I'd remain impassive around you.

Five o'clock runs into eight, so we get up and walk out into the city. We never mention the almost kisses. Your pink lips offered then pulled away. We never mention you laughing and me running, running.

I just stood there, naked, not yet crying, my finger with you all over it, behind my back.

We're standing outside of a bar and you invite me in. Ten o'clock pours into two. We're neither of us drunk, just warm and blurred enough to pretend that we don't know what we're doing. Stopping a cab, you half-sit inside of the open back door, and press your pink fingers against my palm. So like the girl's fingers, but painted now, harder now. Your apartment is right down the street. You pull me in and we pull away.

The apartment is airy and mostly white, including the shamelessly soft carpet. "Must be hell to clean" is all I think, as you walk over, sit on the couch and I follow. Billie Holiday is floating through the walls and window. You watch me until tears start rolling down your cheeks. I wipe them away with my thumbs. Any excuse.

"I haven't got anyone to love me anymore."

"You're crazy. I've always loved you."

I look at my hands. You reach out, grab my ear and hair, and pull me to you. You kiss me. Kiss me, oh, kiss me. Kiss me.

Later in bed you're dark and liquid over me. Your hair wet in all the moonlight. I kiss you down, down, until finally, after twenty years I kiss the other pink place where I've always wanted to touch you. The smell reminds me....

The smell reminds me of that day when my finger smelt almost, but not quite, like this. Less like peaches and more like hay. You sneezed in the dusty quiet of my closet just before they ripped the door open and sunlight splattered in all over us with our underwear off and thrown in the corner. You didn't even look at me but cried and ran to my mother, swearing I had forced you.

Forced you ... My father never before or since hit me as hard as he did that night. His hairy worker hand with its cracked black-rimmed fingernails whistled through the air. I bit down so hard. My mouth was full of blood.

There's blood in my mouth. You don't make a noise, but sit up so fast your stomach smacks against my forehead. You barely push my face away with one limp hand and cup the other over your crotch. You just stare at me. Tears are rolling over your cheeks again, but I can't reach out to you now so they gather under your chin like the ribbons of that blue sailor hat you always wore to church. They drop over your breasts and streak the Chinese symbol on your stomach. I don't know what it means. You gather the blankets around you.

I didn't mean to hurt you.

My father probably said two words to me after that. He could hardly bring himself to look at me. I used to be his favorite. He must have thought not only was I unnatural, I was hell-bent on recruiting the neighbors too.

I didn't mean to hurt you. I leave you there in your bloody blanket mess, taking my unsaid apology with me.

It's three flights down to the street where everything is getting ready for the sunrise. The wind hits me wet and silvery. That voice inside that was silent all night is screaming at me now to turn around and look up at your window. I don't. Instead I cross the nearly empty street and walk through the jingling door of a Chinese grocery. I'm amazed that anything is open so early. I buy a hard red delicious, and after wiping it on my dirty Levis, take a sweet mouthful. The juice gathers on my lips and slips over my chin. I don't bother to wipe it away.

UGLY DUCKLING SYNDROME

My friends called it the "Ugly Duckling Syndrome". I'd considered myself ugly for so long that I just couldn't say no to any guy who showed interest in me. I was so flattered that guys found me attractive! So it started out with me just fooling around with random guys from school, parties, whatever. I didn't complain that they didn't want anything but play from me. (I gave my first hand job before I got my first kiss.) I figured I should take what I could get.

After doing this for a year, I noticed the toll it was taking on me, so I got a real boyfriend. He was sweet and good looking but boring. He cared about me, though. All the same, I just couldn't shake my hooking-up habit. For two months I stayed loyal to him, but slowly I started to get restless. He was so predictable! I stopped partying with him on the weekends and started meeting new guys.

Then, at my first drunken house party (without him) in ages, an ex-fuck buddy of mine showed up. He was looking as hot as ever. I was immediately drawn to him. We hung out the whole night and ended up making out. We had nothing but sexual attraction to each other, which made our affair safe for me emotionally. We used each other. He wanted to cum and I wanted ...validation. I wanted someone else to let me know I'm pretty. It was the ugly duckling syndrome all over again. I didn't feel bad that I was cheating on my boyfriend. I was flattered. I was proud … almost. I felt like I was telling everybody whoever said I was ugly that I wasn't. I didn't just have one guy after me, I had two!

After a while one of my friends talked some sense into me: I was being a bitch to both guys. I swore I'd stop the affair, but the next time I saw my fuck buddy, I just didn't know how to say no. When my boyfriend started to get suspicious, I began to feel guilty (kinda). I decided that if I really cared for my boyfriend, I wouldn't feel the need to cheat, so I dumped him. I also ditched the other guy. It was one of the most liberating experiences I'd had in a while. Having the strength and respect for myself to be without any guy in my life – no boyfriend, no fuck buddy – was amazing. Looking back on our relationship, I feel bad that I cheated so much, and I realize I cheated to bring myself up without even stopping to think how it could've brought other people down, myself included.

—Anonymous, 16

Relationships

The Good, the Bad, and the Bumping Uglies

A healthy relationship makes you *and* your partner feel good about yourselves. Period. Check out these statements and think about which ones apply to your relationship.

THE ISSUE	THE GOOD	THE BAD
How you treat your partner	You are honest about your feelings and you feel comfortable talking with your partner.	You are so worried your partner will leave you that you'll do anything to please him/her.
	You feel happy and safe in your relationship.	Your partner says he/she can't live without you and you're scared that it's true.
How your partner treats you	Your partner respects your feelings.	Your partner regularly puts you down or say things that make you cry.
	Your partner supports your dreams and encourages you to pursue your interests.	You feel ignored, stupid, or unwanted in your relationship.
	Your partner trusts you.	Your partner uses "love" as an excuse for violent or jealous behavior.

THE ISSUE	THE GOOD	THE BAD
Time together	Both of you decide how you spend your time together.	You've had to give up something important to you since you started dating.
Time apart	You still spend time with your family and friends, so that you aren't always with your boy/girl-friend.	Your partner makes you feel guilty if you want your own space.
Time with friends	Your friends say your partner treats you well.	Your partner makes fun of you in front of friends.
Bumping uglies	Your partner makes you feel comfort-able and sexy.	Your partner makes you feel bad if you aren't comfortable doing certain sexual things.
	You and your partner always use protection against STIs and unplanned pregnancy.	You feel pressured by your partner into doing sexual things you're not ready for.

So? Have you got a lot more "good" than "bad"? If so, congrats on being in a healthy relationship. If not, you may be headed for trouble. Check out the resources section at the back of this book if you need more info or someone to talk to.

The Road of Life

People often say somewhere along your road of life you'll find out who your real friends are, but sometimes we don't. I don't think very many people have loyal friends these days. Everyone spends more time back stabbing each other than they do respecting one another. What people should tell you is that somewhere along your road of life you'll find out who YOU really are and discover that sometimes your only true friend is yourself.

Suvi Siu (text and illustration)

Relationship Abuse

Chauntae Walls

What are the different types of relationship abuse?

There are many different kinds of abuse. Some people find some harder to identify than others do. There is the obvious one:

Physical abuse

is when someone physically hurts you, by punching, pushing, slapping, kicking, physically trapping, or hitting with objects. Often the victim is made to feel as though she deserved it. No one deserves to be physically abused.

Emotional and mental abuse

is when someone is controlling you emotionally and mentally, when they manipulate how you feel and use it to their advantage. An example would be if your partner tries to scare you by doing risky things that make you upset, like driving a car too fast, or if your partner is mad at you and tells you they are going to kill themselves because of you, or trying to control how you look and how you feel about yourself.

Mental abuse can be not letting you make decisions for yourself, or controlling how you do things, or what you do with your time. Emotional and mental abuse can be very subtle and often hard to identify. It can leave a person feeling out of control and horrible about themselves and unable to make decisions. Therefore they find it very difficult to change the situation.

Verbal abuse

is when your partner verbally attacks you or constantly puts you down. Verbal abuse can be things like name-calling, put-downs, and screaming. Verbal abuse can make someone lose self-esteem and confidence. It can leave a person feeling worthless and unable to speak up for themself. They start to believe what their partner is saying.

Abuse in same-sex relationships

There is a myth out there that people in same sex-relationships are never abusive. It does exist. *All* types of abuse—from physical to emotional and mental abuse to verbal abuse—can exist in same-sex relationships.

REALITY TV

I am looking for something I do not possess,
my search for happiness is bitter and long
but *The Bold and the Beautiful* must press on
because I am not yet *The Swan*.
Sometimes I think with blond hair, blue eyes
maybe I could have *Friends* too,
meet my own Rachel Ross Joey and Phoebe.
Right now I'm tired of looking in the mirror and
seeing all the mistakes God made
lacking perfection not even an *Extreme Makeover* can create.
But I continue to seek the truth, an inner majesty,
by calling on *Dr. Phil*, somebody help me, please.
I am living, dreaming, wanting to be something but I'm not
I am what I am and am nothing less,
my happiness is not externally defined;
So with each passing day *As the World Turns*,
I dig a little deeper and uncover a little more,
I accept the *Good Times* as they come because,
who doesn't want to be a *Millionaire*, gain a *Queer Eye*
and have a little *Sex in the City* while still *Young and Restless*,
but what it really comes down to is that
I only have *One Life to Live*
and now nearing the end of the *Countdown*
and another year of my life will have been wasted.

Corrine Aberdeen

Suvi Siu

46

Periods

Ahh, yes, that time of the month again. ... Once a month or so we are blessed with the friendly reminder that we have the ability to procreate. As wonderful as this periodic celebration is, it also can be a real pain, physically and otherwise. Periods are a commitment to womanhood that we endure for around forty years—that's A LOT of pads and tampons!! In this chapter you'll find some cool info on the why's and how's of our bleeding bodies.

Chi Nguyen

Emily T.

47

The MENSTRUAL Cycle
The Group

The time from the beginning of one period to the beginning of the next is called the **menstrual cycle**. This cycle lasts an average of **28 days**.

You may notice between periods a wet or dry feeling in your vagina. This wet feeling will probably come a few days after your period ends. You might notice liquidy discharge when you wipe yourself or on your underwear. This fluid may be for cleaning your vagina and cervix, for lubrication during sex, and/or for helping sperm swim into your **womb** (or **uterus**).

Around the middle of your cycle (13 to 15 days before the first day of your next period), the liquidy stuff gets thinner and clearer like raw egg white. At the same time, an **egg** is preparing to move out of your **ovary** (the place in your body that makes the eggs). This is called **ovulation**. After the egg leaves your ovary, it makes its way into the **Fallopian tube**. If a man and a woman have sexual intercourse without birth control (or if the birth control doesn't work – yikes!), a sperm can enter the egg and **fertilization** occurs. The fertilized egg will travel to the womb. The lining of the womb builds up after ovulation, preparing a spongy bed for a fertilized egg. The egg attaches itself to the built-up lining for the nine months it takes to grow a baby.

If the egg isn't fertilized, it still travels along the Fallopian tube, but then dissolves before reaching the womb. Once the egg is gone, the lining isn't needed, so it leaves the body (it looks like blood) – that's your period coming about fourteen days after you ovulate. And then the whole cycle starts again. Cool eh?

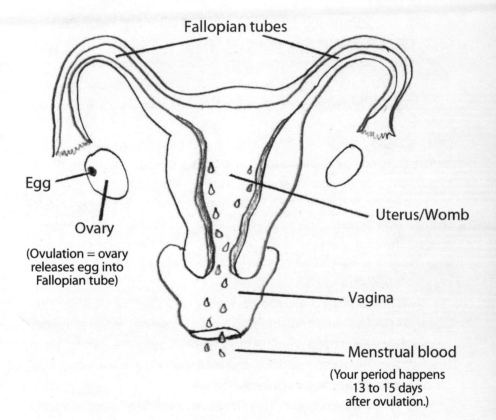

Fallopian tubes

Egg

Ovary

(Ovulation = ovary
releases egg into
Fallopian tube)

Uterus/Womb

Vagina

Menstrual blood

(Your period happens
13 to 15 days
after ovulation.)

BETTER THAN MY OWN

I remember when my friend got her first period better than when I got mine. I can't really remember mine. My period came and went without me ever talking to anyone, other than my friends who were shocked and amazed at how early I got it.

My mother passed by in the kitchen one day, two years after I had gotten it, and she said, "Have you came across your period yet?"

"Yes," I told her and that was that.

The big period talk was over. She had never talked to me about it before then, so I didn't want to talk about it now. Somehow I had known what to do and what my period was all about.

One night my father came into my room and said, "So you're a woman now, sweetie." My eyes squinted my evil squint and I cringed and squirmed under that word: "WOMAN". I felt like he was creeping into something he shouldn't. Somehow that meant something that I really didn't want to be.

My friend got her period at school in grade five. She thought she was dying, in the bathroom, blood running down her leg, soaking her underpants. She started crying and screaming. Someone ran to get a teacher and the teacher came in and took her to the nurse's office. I thought, "It's true, maybe she is gonna die".

You see, no one had ever told her about bleeding, especially from there. It was a shock and a bit of a wake-up call for the teachers to start talking to us about menstruation.

Poor Tina, bloody, screaming Tina. I'm sure at that moment the joy of becoming a woman didn't seem all it was hyped up to be.

Anonymous

photo: Emma Brown

Period Interview

Interview by Suvi Siu with Debbie Garshon, Toronto Health Promoter

Other words for period:
- bleeding
- the curse
- menstruation
- my visiting friend
- rag

Q. Why do women get their first periods at different ages, like 12 or 17?
A. It depends on the woman. Some will physically mature earlier and some will mature later. When her body is ready, it will mature and she'll start having her periods.

Q. What is the normal length of a period?
A. A period usually lasts two to eight days. Shorter than that may only be spotting and not a true period. Longer than eight days would be worth getting checked out by a doctor, especially if the flow is heavy.

Q. Does a tampon make your vagina wider/bigger?
A. No, not at all. The vagina is a flexible passageway. When a tampon (or penis) is inserted, the elastic walls of the vagina stretch to accommodate. When the tampon (or penis) is removed, the vagina returns to its original shape and size.

Q. Can virgins use tampons?

A. Yes, you can certainly use a tampon before you have had penetrative vaginal sex. There is a membrane (piece of skin), called the hymen, which sometimes will block a bit of the opening. Some women won't notice it at all while others might find their vaginal openings tighter. If it is difficult to put a tampon in your vagina, you could try inserting your own fingers to stretch the opening or use a water-based lubricant with the tampon. *(For more info about hymens, see page 69.)*

Q. What does it mean when your period is late and you are not pregnant?

A. It could mean a few things. If you're definitely not pregnant it could just mean it's delayed. Some women's periods will be delayed because of stress and body changes like weight loss, weight gain, illness, or changes in lifestyle. It's not uncommon to miss a period every once in a while, especially when you first start getting it. It doesn't necessarily mean there is anything wrong with you; your body just might be off one month. That said, if it continues for two to three months in a row, then you should talk to a doctor.

Q. Do you weigh more before your period and less after?

A. Some women do tend to retain water – this is called bloating. It's very common and, therefore, you might weigh 454–908 g (1–2 lb.) more. Once your period is completed, that water retention goes away. We call this cyclical weight gain: around your cycle you'll gain then lose and gain then lose it.

Q. Should you use a tampon or a pad?

A. It's really a personal decision. Some women don't like to use tampons and for them a pad would be better. Some women hate pads. A number of women use both if their periods are really heavy, or they may alternate. Other women use alternative methods like reuseable pads and menstrual cups. *(See pages 57–61 for more info.)*

Dysmenorrhea

The Group

Many women suffer from painful periods. "Dysmenorrhea" is the medical term for that abdominal pain that is sharp and crampy. Sometimes you also get back pain, diarrhea, vomiting, and headaches. It is thought that dysmenorrhea is caused by a hormone-like substance in our bodies that can cause pain. This substance—called a big ol' word: "prostaglandin"—helps your body contract its muscles in your uterus. Too much of this stuff makes for serious period cramps: they are longer and tighter and very painful. The pain you feel is from your muscles not getting oxygen, which is kinda like they are temporarily suffocating—which HURTS.

So take deep, deep breaths and do everything you can do to relax your muscles. Try a hot water bottle on your belly or back or a hot bath. Or stretch, go for a walk, masturbate, or have a massage done on your lower belly and lower back. Experiment to figure out what helps YOU relax.

You can also try over-the-counter pain medication such as ibuprofen. If you have really bad pain, see a doctor. They can prescribe medication that helps.

Rebecca Hodgson-Dewitt

When your monthly visitor isn't a monthly visitor

Each woman is unique and so, of course, each woman's menstrual cycle Is also unique. Some females will have very regular cycles, while others don't follow the 28-day textbook standard. An irregular cycle does not necessarily mean anything, especially within a year of your first period. If you were sexually active after your last period and now you're waiting for a period that just won't show up, then there is the possibility that you're pregnant. Best to get a pregnancy test to be sure! BUT pregnancy is not always the reason; your period can also be delayed by stress, strict diet, side effects of medications, and in a few cases, diseases such as polycystic ovary disease (multiple cysts on the ovary). So if you've ruled out pregnancy and you've been studying really hard, or desperately trying to lose weight, relax and eat a burger (or your preferred junk food) and let the good times flow.
However, if the problem persists and you've previously had a regular menstrual cycle for over a year, you should definitely visit your doctor.

Corrine Aberdeen

the Dispenser.

Arghhh ... TAMPONS?!?!?

Corrine Aberdeen

With each passing day leading up to your period, the question "what should I wear, hmmm ... pad or tampon?" pops up. Many women compare wearing a pad to wearing a diaper, but tampons also have their pros and cons. Pros include that they're very discreet—you can even go swimming. Cons include the risk of toxic shock syndrome (TSS), which has been linked to tampon use. TSS is caused by bacteria that thrives in the environment created by a tampon being in your body for too long. To prevent TSS, you should change your tampon every four to eight hours and choose the correct absorbency (light to heavy) for that day. If, while wearing a tampon, you experience ...

- sudden high fever
- sunburn-like rash
- diarrhea
- dizziness/light-headedness/fainting
- vomiting

... be sure to immediately remove the tampon and go straight to your doctor. TSS is quite rare, though it can be very serious if it goes untreated.

Tampons are worth trying at least once, maybe on a day when you have lots of time to get comfortable with it, that way you have less to worry about.

TAMPONS

A How-To

by Suvi Siu

So, ever heard of tampons? Not too sure you want to try them? You're scared of the damn things? You think the idea of putting something up your vagina is gross? Well, guess what? Let me tell you something: they're not all that bad!

I know they may sound scary, weird, or disgusting, but once you've tried using them you may never want to go back to pads. Once you put a tampon in properly you can't even feel it ! You feel like going out more, you can run, you can go swimming (which you can't do while using a pad), you can play sports, heck, you can even dance and exercise! Of course, you can still do activities while wearing a pad, but, in my opinion, a tampon is much more comfortable and much more protective. Just because you are on your period doesn't mean you can't go out and have fun. Don't let it hold you down. Yes, I know, sure you can sit home all day in PJs watching TV and eating junk food, and maybe for some people that's what they feel like doing when they are on their period, but wouldn't you rather get out of the house?

Putting in a tampon is not that hard. If it is your first time you may be scared. My first time putting in a tampon I was so scared and nervous, but once I had it in I was so happy. There was no more going to the bathroom every 20 minutes, no more messiness, no more walking weirdly, and best of all, no more feeling the blood coming out.

When you are putting a tampon in, it is best to stay calm and relaxed and try not to be nervous. **Here, I'll show you how to put in a tampon properly:**

THESE ARE INSTRUCTIONS FOR TAMPONS WITH APPLICATORS.

Unwrap the tampon. Put one foot up with your knee bent.

Feel for your vaginal hole. This is the opening between your legs closer to the front of your body rather than the hole in your bum.

Push the tampon until your fingers holding the middle of the tampon touch the outside of your body. Try to keep it on an upward angle towards the small of your back. Everyone's vagina and cervix are on a different angle.

With your index finger, push the smaller part of the applicator up into the larger part (see picture). This will slide the tampon out of the applicator.

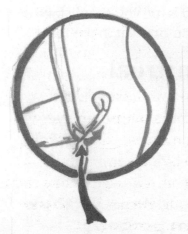

Remove applicator, leaving the tampon inside. Leave the string hanging out. The tampon cannot get lost inside. If the string is not there (which almost never happens!), you may have to feel inside your vagina and fish it out.

If it feels uncomfortable, or like it is falling out, then it is not far enough up. In this case, pull the tampon out and try again with a new tampon.

When you are ready to pull it out, be aware that, if it is at the end of your period, the tampon might be dry and hard to get out. Don't panic: relax and pull gently.

If you've tried tampons and pads and you don't like them, but you feel like you're stuck with them, why not consider some alternatives?

There is something called a menstrual cup. A menstrual cup is sort of like a tampon but not really. It's shaped like a little cup. It sits inside your vagina under your cervix like a bowl and catches all of your period blood. Once the cup is full you simply take it out (while standing over the toilet) and dump it in the toilet, rinse it off and reuse it again. The menstrual cup is great for the environment because you don't have to constantly throw out tampons, adding to all the garbage our world already has. If you are a person who is really concerned about the environment, then the

menstrual cup

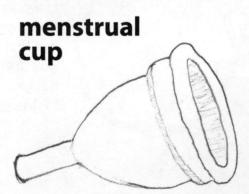

menstrual cup is for you! There are two major brands of menstrual cup: the Keeper is made of rubber latex and the DivaCup is made of silicone. They can be found at health food stores. Check out the resources section for where to find more info.

There are also reusable pads. A reusable pad, is just a pad made out of terry cloth or flannel fabric. Once you've used the pad you simply wash it, let it dry, and use it again. It's another good product for the environment.

If you check out these alternatives and find the one that works best for you, I promise you, you'll discover that having your period isn't such a bad thing after all. You may think it's a drag but really it's not that bad. Hey, if you never had your period you wouldn't be able to have babies when you're older!

I hate tampons!

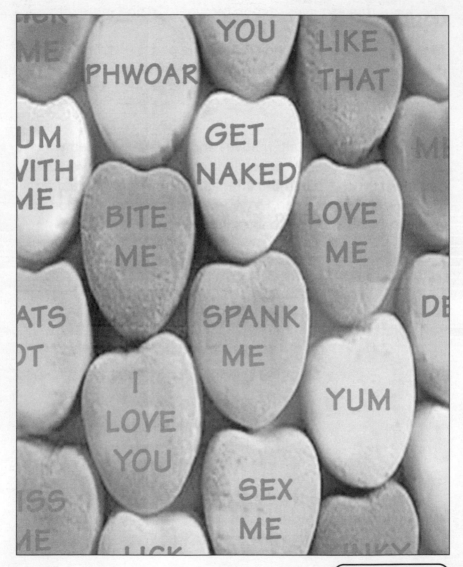

Imogen Birchard

SEX

Chapter 3

A short three letter word that can completely change your life ...

sex. Discovering your sexuality occurs at very different points in different people's lives. Whether you're straight, bisexual, or lesbian, sex can be a really confusing, overwhelming, and fun. Whether or not you choose to participate in sexual activity, you need to know that it's something that you actively choose to do. No one should impose their wants on you. So, here it is. A whole chapter about sex.

Chi Nguyen

Jessica J.

SeX sEx SEX

Hilary Quigley

> Having sex *is* a very big deal, and *if* you are
> going to have it, or you are having it,
> you have to make sure it's good for you.

There are a whole bunch of things that come along with sex that a lot of people don't think carefully about before jumping in. **Along with the stuff that feels good, sex comes with a whole big package of things to worry about, like condoms, birth control, AIDS, STIs, lies, pregnancy, and a whole lot of other shit.** Even when people do know about these risks, they sometimes just choose to ignore them. It's like the word "sex" is one huge carpet and all the dirty, messy stuff gets swept underneath it. What we have to realize is that we can't just sweep everything away; we need to hear about it and deal with the fact that sex is more than taking off your pants and enjoying yourself.

So, if you're going to have sex, there are things you really need to know. Learn about STIs and birth control so you know how to protect yourself physically. It could be your life on the line. Talk to your partner, your friends, and anyone you trust to prepare yourself emotionally. It could also be your heart on the line.

Pain LIES PREGNANCY Women
FRIENDS STD'S BOYS
Girls worries
MEN
Sex
Fear GERMS
Babies DEATH Condoms
infections AIDS LOVE
Birth control

Suvi Siu

Remember that growing up, you took steps, steps like learning how to ride a bike for the first time, walking to school all by yourself, or learning how to ride the subway alone. When you get to the point in your life when you're ready to have sex, it's not a step anymore, it's like a huge jump—a jump that may take you to the other side or you may just fall in the middle, straight down, landing on your butt. Learn everything you can before you leap and you'll be better off however you land.

The first time I had sex

The first time I had sex was an amazing experience.
My boyfriend and I had talked a couple times about having sex.

We both seemed eager, but we both agreed to wait until the time came, whenever it felt right for both of us. We had been going out for about two or three weeks and we'd known each other pretty well before.

In our first week dating, he told me one night that he loved me. I was surprised, but I loved him too and I told him. We spent lots of time together in the next couple of weeks. We fell completely in love with each other. Then after spending the day with him and a couple of friends, he and I were lying on my bed kissing. I kept thinking about having sex with him. I knew this was the right time, and before I could say anything, he said that he loved me and asked if we could have sex.

I was completely into it—I was relaxed, we were using a condom, and I knew the person I was with was the right person.

Afterwards we held each other and I felt so good about it and it hadn't even hurt.

My boyfriend and I continued to have a meaningful and very fun sex life for the next five months.

Even though we broke up and we never speak or even look at each other anymore, and I've had sex with different people since him, I'm glad he was my first. I don't regret it and I'll always remember it.

First

I always dreamed I'd have an amazing orgasm the first time I had sex. My actual first time was nothing like my fantasy, but I still enjoyed it because I was with a guy I loved. It was a cold November night and we were messing around and he asked if we could have sex. I wanted to, so we found a condom and had sex for maybe 10 minutes.

He came, I didn't. It was not painful. I think because I was relaxed and in love. We did it a second time 5 minutes later for a little longer. It was beautiful and I loved it. I did not come, but he did again. After that first time, we started to have sex pretty often. I was always always careful. I went to the doctor every 3 - 4 months and most importantly I ALWAYS used a condom.

Eventually, somewhere along the way, I lost my boyfriend along with my respect for myself. Sex meant nothing to me again. This continued for a while until I eventually learned that I couldn't have sex unless I had respect for myself. I learned that an important part about having sex with someone is that there must be communication and trust (and protection!). If there isn't any of these things, what is the point? In the end you'll be hurt and have less respect for yourself, which is not something you should put yourself through.

I am at a point in my life now where sex is about love, respect, pleasure, and trust. It's about being with someone who I am in love with and who's in love with me. It is something I will share only with one person (my boyfriend) and it will stay between us forever.

Remember, even if you aren't with someone forever, it doesn't mean you can't remember how much fun you had in the sack. For me, sex means that it is my own definition, my choice whether to have it or not. It means that it belongs to me and no one can take that away

Anonymous, 17

67

SEX Interview

Information taken from interviews with
Karen Arthurton (from YOUTHLINK Inner City) and
Bridget Sinclair, Youth Services Worker, St. Stephen's Community House
Written by Emma Brown

Other words for sex:
- bouncing
- doggy style
- screwing
- intercourse
- get laid
- getting me some
- missionary
- shagging
- slipping in the back door

Q. What is sex?

A. Sex is sex is sex is sex? There are a lot of different definitions for "sex". For some people it can be fondling, hugging, and kissing. For others it is eating someone out or a blow job (oral sex), fingering, or hand jobs. Still others insist it is penetration, penis in vagina, penis in anus, or dildo in vagina. There is no one single definition that accurately includes every type of sex.

Q. When is it a good time to have sex?

A. This is a very difficult question. It really depends on the individual. A person has to ask herself a lot of questions: Does it feel right? Are you emotionally ready? Are you physically ready? Have you thought about safe sex and birth control? Do you trust the person you're with? Is it something you want to do, or are you feeling pressured by friends or your partner? No one can tell you when it's the right time.

Q. What is a hymen and what does it have to do with being a virgin?

A. When you are born, there is a thin membrane (like a piece of thin skin) that partially or completely covers the opening of the vagina. Hymens are different on every woman. People assume that the first time you have sex your hymen is broken, and that when the hymen is broken, you'll bleed. But sometimes a girl's hymen has already been broken during bike-riding or horseback-riding or other sports. Just because a young woman doesn't bleed the first time she has sex doesn't mean that she wasn't a virgin.

Q. The first time you have sex, will it hurt?

A. It depends, because all of us are so different. For a lot of women, it does hurt. It's pretty hard to feel relaxed when it's your first time and you don't know what to expect. If you are tense and/or scared, it may hurt. But that may not be the case for everybody. Some girls may find that their first time doesn't hurt at all. Or it may just be slightly uncomfortable for a short time. If the first time is forced, it's probably going to hurt.

Q. How can you say no to sex?

A. You can say it verbally. You can also let someone know with your actions. Whenever somebody says no, it needs to be respected by the other person. The best way to say no is to say it clearly, loudly, and strongly—**"NO!"** Try to look the person in the eye when you say it.

Q. Where can you go to talk about sex?

A. If you can't talk to your friends or your parents, or you want more information, you could go to a local community center. Many community centers have youth departments that will have healthy sexuality information. See additional resources at the back of this book.

If you are thinkin' that you're ready to have sex, go through these question to think about how ready you really are.

1. Do you have a partner to have sex with?

2. Do you love yourself? ➡️

> Do you treat yourself well? Do you take care of yourself? Do you make sure you put yourself in healthy, safe situations? Your relationship with yourself is really the most important and should always be first priority. If you don't know who you are and haven't formed a good relationship with yourself, then how will you know how to be healthy with someone else?

Emma Brown

Are You Ready to Have Sex?

3. Do you respect yourself? ➡️

> You have to respect yourself the same way you respect your friends and other people in your life.

4. Do you respect your partner?

5. Does your partner respect you?

6. Do you trust your partner?

7. Does your partner pressure you into moving too fast?

> It is pressure if your boy or girl tells you that "if you love me, then you would have sex with me," or if they make you feel uptight or scared if you don't move faster and farther. It is pressure if they get angry when you don't want to go further.

8. Have you talked with your partner about sex?

9. Have you both talked about protection and do you have some?

10. Do you want to have sex?

> If you do have doubts, it doesn't mean that you shouldn't have sex, but it does mean that you should think about what your doubts are, and what you want to do about them.

11. Do you FEEL ready?

12. Do you have any doubts?

13. Can you talk to your partner about your doubts?

14. Are you having sex for the right reasons?

> What are the right reasons: It's something you want to do; you feel comfortable and safe. You feel respected by the person. You feel turned on by the person. You're attracted to the person and care about them. You're comfortable and excited about moving forward.

In the end you should have sex because you want to. No one can ever tell you when it is a good time to have sex; only you will know what's right for you.
If you are uncomfortable about any of your answers to these questions, then maybe you should just wait. What's the rush? Waiting is never a bad thing.

Know yourself and what's good for you. You come first !!

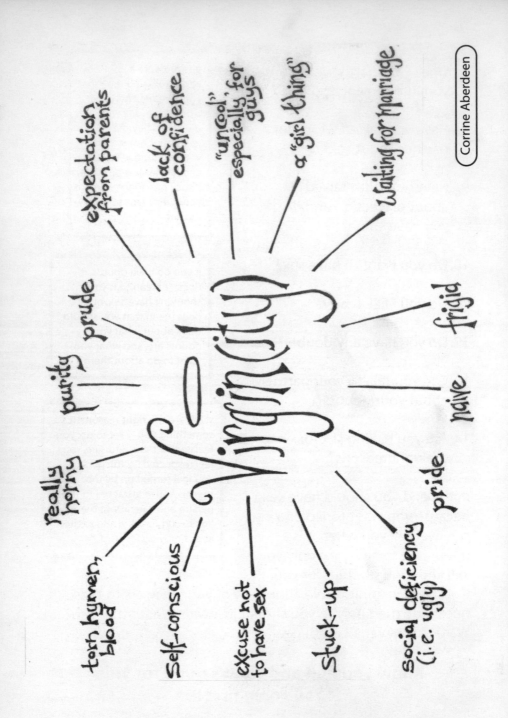

Virgin(ity)

expectation from parents

lack of confidence

"uncool", especially for guys

a "girl thing"

Waiting for Marriage

prude

purity

really horny

frigid

naïve

pride

torn hymen, blood

self-conscious

excuse not to have sex

stuck-up

social deficiency (i.e. ugly)

Corrine Aberdeen

Confessions of a Virgin

Virgin ...

It's never had a negative connotation in my mind, never been something to be ashamed of being, but at the same time not something I'd brag about. I don't hide the fact. It's not like I'm waiting for something or somebody; I just don't see the rush. Maybe it's my overall lack of intimacy, relationships, or sex drive. I'm never the pursuer in relationships, actually I quite like pushing people away. Sometimes I feel like a bit of a sexual leper. Do I want sex? The thought rarely crosses my mind. I hate the thought of being connected to someone by a contract our bodies agree on ... to be honest it scares me.

Sometimes I think I'm waiting for the person who will help me overcome my fear and maybe that's when I'll progress, change, experience the birds and the bees instead of just writing about them. I always imagine my first time as being something special and I'm sure it'll be great when it happens and I'll probably be easily impressed.

Well that's enough from me for today ... I'll let you know if anything *special* happens.

Anonymous

73

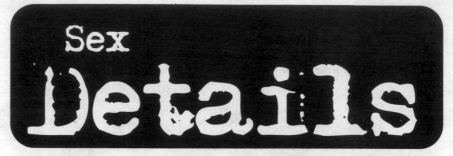

Sex Details

Questions and answers compiled from the Arcade Down & Dirty discussion group facilitated by Jessica Harrod and Bridget Sinclair, Youth Services Workers, St. Stephen's Community House

Q. What is good sex?
A. If you ask different women, you'll get different responses. Individuals have different sexual tastes, which is why it's important to talk about what you like and don't like. That's hard because it's difficult sometimes to talk about sex. If you're young, you may not know what you like, so it's important to get to know your own body. One way to do that is through masturbation.

But the key to good sex is respect. For sex to be good, both partners should be satisfied and happy. There should be some talk about what each person likes and doesn't like and about how to make it safer so you're not worrying about unwanted pregnancy or disease. Good sex is not forced or pressured. People involved in good sex are doing it because they want to do it, and not because everyone else is. Sex should make you feel good about yourself, and not leave you feeling shameful or used.

Q. Do you have to be in love?
A. No. Lots of people have sex when they aren't in love. There's nothing wrong with sexual expression; it's part of who you are. The important thing about sex is that it should never be forced and should always be respectful.

Q. Is it bad to sleep with lots of people?
A. Once again, ask yourself if it's respectful sex. Is the person protecting herself against STIs and pregnancy? Does she feel okay emotionally? Is she doing it because other people are doing it, or because she thinks

it's cool? Keep in mind too that, although they may look fully mature on the outside, young women are still developing inside. Having many partners or having sex really early can put them at greater risk of contracting STIs. And remember, if you're not doing it at all, that's OK too. It's fine to be a virgin. It's also fine to decide, after having sex, that it's not what you want right now. You don't have to keep having sex just because you did once.

Q. What is a blow job?
A. A blow job is performing oral sex (using your mouth) on a guy's penis.

When you give head to guy you may lick his penis and balls. You may want to suck on his penis and use your hand on the shaft. The head of the penis is very sensitive and is a good area to play with the pressure of your tongue. Slowing down and speeding up your hand will also help him to orgasm. You will want to use a condom to protect yourself from STIs and HIV/AIDS.

At no point do you have to swallow the cum (a.k.a semen—the white stuff, usually less than one teaspoon, that ejaculates out of the guy's penis) or even let him cum in your mouth. You can spit it out or pull away and use your hand before he cums.

The most important thing is that you are both communicating about what you are comfortable with and what feels good. I would suggest that, when you give a blow job, you have the guy lie down so you can control how deep his penis goes into your mouth/throat. Remember that you have the right to decide what type of sex you have; you don't have to have oral sex.

Q. How do you have oral sex with a girl?
A. When you are eating out a girl you may want to lick and gently suck on the clitoris and the labia. You may want to gently use your fingers in her vagina. You can speed up and play with the pressure of your tongue on her clitoris to help her to achieve an orgasm. Again the most important part is that you are communicating about what feels good and what is comfortable. Often people find it difficult to find the clitoris, remember to ask! You will need to discuss with your partner the use of a dental dam (see Chapter 8) to help protect you from STIs and HIV/AIDS.

Q. What are guys' areas of pleasure?
A. The head of the penis is a sensitive part for men. A guy will be sensitive in other areas as well, but this varies from guy to guy. Talking to your partner is very important since people have different likes and dislikes.

Q. If you swallow cum, will it do anything to you?
A. You cannot get pregnant, but it is possible to get some STIs if you swallow cum. It's considered a low-risk activity for transmitting the HIV virus. That means it is not as risky as unprotected vaginal or anal intercourse. The risk of oral sex depends on the condition of your throat and mouth. Some people use a condom for oral sex. You will have to decide what level of risk you are willing to take.

Q. Does anal sex hurt more then vaginal sex?
A. Some people find anal sex pleasurable and erotic. Some people don't. Because the anus doesn't have natural lubricants like the vagina, using lube is a good idea. Like vaginal intercourse, if you're tense, it's going to hurt. And like vaginal intercourse, there may be a certain amount of discomfort at first before it gets pleasurable. It may feel better if the penis goes in a little bit at a time rather than going in really quick. Remember that anal sex is a high-risk activity in terms of infections and disease. The lining of the rectum tears more easily than the vagina. If the skin breaks and there is bleeding, the possibilty of transmission increases. Use condoms!

Q. Are there different types of orgasms?
A. Yes, there are different types of orgasms. Some are quick, while some can be longer. Some are very intense, while some are gentler. Women can have what you call multiple orgasms; that's when you can have one after another after another. An orgasm from oral sex may feel different from a vaginal sex orgasm, which may feel different from an orgasm achieved with a vibrator. A woman can have one on her own through masturbation or with a partner. Some women have difficulty having an orgasm. It doesn't mean that they are frigid or are poor lovers.

Orgasms will vary from person to person. Some people will breathe hard, while others will hold their breath. Some people will feel a rush of heat to their face. Generally, it's a feeling of buildup and release and pleasure.

When a woman is excited, her clitoris actually swells. Sometimes she may feel her vaginal lips contracting during an orgasm. After an orgasm, she may find that her clitoris is very sensitive and she may not want to be touched again too soon.

Q. Does your ability to have an orgasm depend on your emotional mood?
A. Certainly it depends on your mood. There may be times when you know that it's just not going to happen. You may be into it emotionally but not physically. Other times your body may respond even when you don't want it to. That doesn't mean that you secretly want it to happen, it just means your body is responding physically. Listen to what you are feeling.

We should remember that a lot of girls and women have had negative sexual experiences that can make it difficult to enjoy sex. Please read the sexual assualt chapter (Chapter 9) for more information.

My First Time Sexing a Girl

When I was 15 years old, I tried out for the Junior Girls' Volleyball team and became co-captain with another girl. I had seen her around school but never dared to approach her, as she was in grade 11, a year ahead of me. Right away she seemed really cool, a truly honest and completely captivating person. Despite my awe of this older girl, she seemed to like me as a person, too.

Over the volleyball season, we became closer and talked about all sorts of crazy stuff, like being attracted to another girl. The thought had never really crossed my mind but she was always totally blunt about her feelings and slowly I realized that our cute little mind games were actually HARD-CORE FLIRTING!

She was going out with the high school basketball star at the time and was therefore involved. Her interest in him existed on nothing more than a sexual level. As a crazy bold move, out of pure curiosity and frustration, I wrote her a letter expressing everything she made me feel: the butterflies in my stomach, wanting to touch her face, the uncontrollable smiles we sported in each other's presence, and the intense conversations we held with our eyes.

She read all of my emotions in the letter in front of me and gave me a look to die for once she finished reading. We sat up with candles in her sister's room and didn't touch, but talked about the entire flirting process. Unfortunately it was a school night, so I left for my house at about 11:30 p.m. I literally skipped through the slushy February streets, laughing out loud. When I got home I was soaked up to my waist.

"Oh, so this is what two girls do together ...hmmm ..."

Our volleyball team kept winning (led by two very close captains) and somehow our curiosity turned into a relationship. On Valentine's Day, she was supposed to go out with the basketball player but in the end she came over to my house for a sleepover!

She offered her services and I obviously complied.

I didn't really think about sex until we got into our pajamas. I had a waterbed at the time (which seems even more hilarious now) and as I recall, two people in it sort of rolled together into the centre.

After a long day, the best thing you can do for a hardworking volleyball player is give her a massage. She offered her services and I obviously complied. When I returned the favor, she pulled the back of her shirt over her head, completely exposing her back to me. At the time, the only coherent thought I remember having was, "Woah."

This girl had a very nice back and being so bold, I leaned down to kiss it and continued to do so until she pulled her shirt down and turned around to face me. I kissed her face all over, avoiding her lips until she moved her lips into the path of mine.

**AAAAAAAAHHHHHHHHHHHHH!!!!!!!!!!!!!!!!!
I'M KISSING A GIRL!!!!!!!**

We were both really into the moment and didn't really stop to question anything. The sexual intensity continued to heighten until I realized, "Oh, so this is what two girls do together ... hmmm ...."

I had my first orgasm on Valentine's Day and was so blown away by the experience that I grabbed my asthma inhaler immediately afterwards. "Are you okay?" she exclaimed. She dumped the jock a few days later and I was very pleased.

It was a total blast. I don't remember feeling scared or nervous in a negative way at all. The only change I would've made would be to ask, "Uh, do you have any STIs?" before we slept together. I was very lucky, I had a really positive first same-sex experience that continued into a six-month relationship, until she moved away that summer for a year.

Now, almost three years later, we aren't screwing, but she's one of my best friends and we maintain a unique connection I feel we won't lose.

We used to joke about our chance encounter in each other's lives when we could have just as easily ended up sleeping with some older dyke living with five cats. The most important part of the whole situation was that we both felt so good and comfortable together that any sort of apprehension was turned into positive anticipation.

Many young women have truly negative first experiences with other girls—at a party on a dare from some horny teenage boy or with someone a lot older than them.

I can only tell my tale and encourage young women to write scandalous letters and flirt with the basketball star's girlfriend and ask those shocking questions! Be sure of your motives and when you track down that cute girl you wanna smooch, make sure you're both completely comfortable. Other than that, have fun, and be careful if you have asthma.

Anonymous, 18

How to talk to your partner about sex!

One of the most important things in a relationship is communication. Knowing how to talk to your partner can be really difficult and kinda scary—especially about S E X. You need to ask yourself this question: if you aren't comfortable talkin' to your guy or girl about sex, then why are you havin' sex with them?!

It's really hard to talk to somebody about sex when you are going hot and heavy, so most people just go with stuff even if they are not into it. This is why it is sooooo important to talk about what you think about sex and what you are comfortable with and what you aren't comfortable with BEFORE you have sex.

If you are ready to have sex but are having trouble getting over the hump of bringing up the topic, or if you are already having sex and there are things that need talking about, here are some suggestions for how to start a conversation about SEX!

+ Do whatever you need to feel comfortable. You could start by making a joke or casual reference to something related to sex to get on the topic.

+ Use props, man!! Have a magazine with a condom ad in it, a book that has some cheesy information for teens about sexuality. Say "Hey did you see this?" or "What do you think?" or something to that effect.

+ Read an article or pamphlet about it together. They are pretty helpful and funny. Once you get the ball rolling it gets easier.

+ Sometimes it's less awkward to broach the topic when you're in a group. You don't have to get into specifics. You could all just talk about your opinion on different types of sex or birth control. It depends on how comfortable you are with your friends. If you'll be able to talk with them, it can make talking to your partner later less scary and you also won't feel so isolated.

+ You could go to a clinic, or drop-in center, with your partner and talk to knowledgeable people there.

+ You could try talking to your partner before, during, or after having sex. You could say things like:
> "This is what I am comfortable with ..."
> "I want to do it like this ..."
> "I like this/that ... that's good ... ahh that's not quite what I like. It would be better if you did this ...."

+ If you want to talk about your partner's techniques, starting with positive reinforcements is a good idea. You don't want to insult your partner. And remember: they probably don't really know what they are doing and need your help! If you want to discourage something specific, it's a good idea to also think of something you want to encourage and say something like, "I'd like more of this and less of this."

These are just suggestions and ideas. You may find some helpful and others not. You may find none of them helpful, but they may help you think of other things. Regardless of how you do it, I hope you can get open communication with your partner. Hey, for me, and for many others I know, communicative sex equals more enjoyable, safe sex. Good luck and have fun!

Annie Grainger

Letz Talk About Sex!

Penny Nicholls

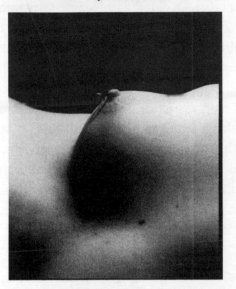

Being sexually active can raise a lotta questions. So where do you go for the answers? Books, music, movies, magazines, the internet, ... but what about your girl friends? They've got answers – they're not right, they're not wrong but they are from their own experiences!

Advice and opinions from other girls can really clear your mind. Did I do it right? Did he do it right? What else can we do? You'd be surprised how knowledgeable you all are and how much you can teach each other, just by talking. I think it's extremely important for friends to share their sexual experience, preferences, concerns, and questions. But do teenage girls talk about sex? It depends on the friendship.

My ex-best friend was extremely shy and self-conscious. I asked her a few questions about sex during our relationship, but her answers were always minimal. I could tell she was uncomfortable with the topic so I stopped bringing it up, even though it would have been interesting for me to compare our first times, to see if hers was pleasurable or painful, if she was happy or scared.

My relationship with my current best friend is SOO the opposite. We talk about our sexual interests and experiences in detail because both of us are completely comfortable with our sexuality and each other. When I say detail, I mean detail: size, length, strength, position, kinky, sweet, rough, soft ... everything! We don't talk every time we engage in a sexual act with someone, but we do discuss the times worth talking about or the times that were kind of weird, when advice and opinions from a girlfriend can help clear up our questions or concerns.

Well, that's my experience, I've had both types of friendships and I'm so happy I have someone to talk with now. If you're close to and comfortable with a friend, why not bring up sex next time you talk? It may seem weird at first, you may feel sort of uncomfortable, but with time that will start to go away. You'll be surprised not only how much she has to offer you, but what you have to offer her. Sex is a wonderful thing ... so is talking about it.

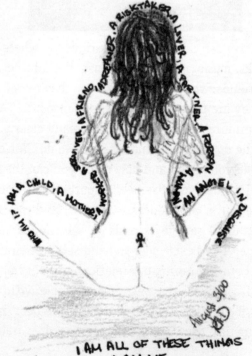

I AM ALL OF THESE THINGS
I AM ME

Chi Nguyen

Sexual Pressure

Most of my girlfriends have been pressured sexually into things they didn't want to do or weren't ready for. This is really horrible.

Most girls think that, if a guy does pressure her, she'll know what to do, she'll be able to handle it without any trouble. But when the time comes, many girls often just go through with it, even though they don't want to.

Speaking from experience, sometimes it is really hard to say no.

No matter how strong you think you are, when a guy starts talking and trying to convince you, it's hard to stand strong, and to know what to say or how to say it, for fear of rejection, for fear something worse could happen.

So girls, when a guy is pressuring you, stay strong. You say "NO", get up, and walk away. If he says it's over or anything else, he's not worth your time. Any guy who can't respect what you want isn't worth it. You can always find someone new and better.

My heart goes out to any girl who's been put in that position. Remember that sex belongs to you and that no stupid guy can steal that from you. **STAY STRONG!!!**

Sexual Stereotyping

slut
ho
bitch

We all know these names; most of us have been called them lots of times. We all know what they mean, but most of us don't know why we are called them. It's like, if a guy has sex, oh boy, he's a player, he's the man, he's all cool 'n' shit, but if a girl goes out and does it, she's a slut. Hell, she don't even have to have sex to be labeled a slut or ho. She can get that label just from her clothes and how she wears her makeup 'n' shit. People label girls like this to bring them down, to make sure she ain't all that, you know what I'm sayin'? People get scared of girls who flaunt it, girls get jealous, and guys get threatened. Guys are supposed to be the only ones who are into sex, who want sex. Girls are supposed to act all shy 'n' shit. That's a bad rap, man. I ain't lettin' no guy want it from me. I'll want it when I want it —and that doesn't make me a slut or ho.

Kalyah Recino, 15

Abstinence

Having sex is a personal choice; therefore not having sex is also a personal choice. Abstinence is when you choose to not do something for a period of time. People's level of sexual abstinence can vary from not having any kind of sexual activity to only abstaining from sexual intercourse.

There are a lot of reasons why people choose to be abstinent. A lot of people abstain for religious or spiritual reasons or because they feel safer and better protected from HIV/AIDS, other STIs, and unplanned pregnancies. Some people don't feel emotionally ready or emotionally satisfied by sex. Some people choose not to have sex because they want to put their energy into other things.

These are all good reasons when you make a decision about sex. You can easily be in a loving, passionate relationship and not be having sex. There are a lot of other ways to show someone that you care about them. You can be affectionate, caring, fun, supportive, and a good listener. You can also tell them how much you care about them.

Remember: sex is not love. They are two separate things and people get confused about them being the same thing.

Susan Chow, 16

You've got this thing that really makes me HOT!

Jumping from bed to bed My name is

and they all hate me now

And now I am nothing

but something to make fun of

Emma Brown

FUN Alternatives to Intercourse

There are a lot of ways to have sex. If you think sex is just intercourse, or screwing, that's where you're wrong! There are many other fun, intimate things you can do together. Lots of women find intercourse overrated, and only about pleasuring the guy. For most women, other stimulation is far, far more enjoyable.

Things like:

* 69ing
* Cyber sex
* Fingering
* Fondling, groping
* Grinding
* Hand jobbing
* Kissing, making out
* Massaging
* Oral sex (going down on each other)
* Petting
* Phone sex

Annie Grainger and Fox F

Check the glossary at the back of the book for more info on these terms.

P.S. You never have to follow through on any sexual activity. If you want to stop, then stop!!

YOU CAN ALWAYS BAIL!!!!

masturbation

I can't remember the first time I did it. My mom said I touched myself as soon as I could reach. As I grew up, I learned to be ashamed. In books and sex education class, everyone always said it was "perfectly normal." How can something be "perfectly normal," if no one ever talks about it? I came to a point in my life where I stopped doing it because I wanted to be what I thought was "truly normal." I never talked to anyone about it until last summer. A fantastic person, who became a good friend, was the first person I ever spoke a word to about my personal experiences with masturbating. Talking to someone for the first time was a huge, difficult step that I'll never forget.

Last fall I was in a relationship with someone who couldn't find a way to pleasure me and desperately wanted pointers. I came to realize that I couldn't tell him what gave me pleasure if I didn't know. So I started to masturbate again. Now I know that I am healthy, strong, powerful, and deserve to be comfortable with my body and experience sexual pleasure free from guilt.

Anonymous, 15

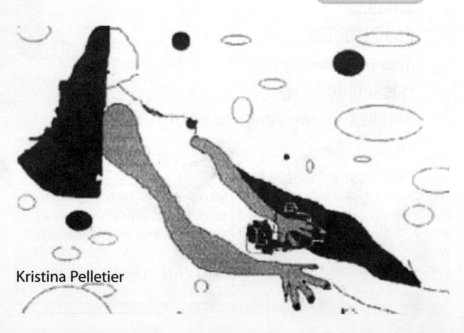

Kristina Pelletier

Masturbation Interview

Interview by Annie Grainger with Sarah Forbes-Roberts from Come As You Are , a co-operatively owned healthy sexuality store in Toronto

Masturbation is an important part of developing your sexuality. As children, touching and playing with your body and vagina is normal. As we grow older, some of us may learn from parents, school, and religion that masturbating is not OK. By the time most people become teenagers, they think that masturbation is bad.

Masturbation is actually normal and healthy. It helps us to understand our own bodies and what make us feel good. Knowing how to give ourselves sexual pleasure brings us freedom. When we enter a relationship, we are not dependent on our partners to satisfy us. We know more about our own bodies, how they work, and what turns us on.

Q: HOW DO YOU MASTURBATE?
A: If you have never tried masturbating, you may feel awkward, self conscious, or maybe a bit scared. Find a quiet place where you can be by yourself. Rub your body with cream or oil or something that feels good. Explore your body, touch yourself in different ways. If you want, think about people and situations that turn you on.

There are many different ways you can masturbate, by rubbing your clitoris with wet fingers, for example. Try different positions or speeds. Some women cross their legs and move muscles around to put pressure on the entire vagina and labia, others may insert something into their vagina, such as a finger or a dildo. Some women rub their breasts. Some use a pillow between their legs or a shower massager.

Q: WHY WOULD SOMEONE MASTURBATE WHEN THEY COULD HAVE SEX?

A. I think having sex with someone else is very different than masturbating alone. It's all about learning about your own body and being alone when you masturbate. Having sex is so often about the other person; masturbating is all about you.

Q: WHY IS IT IMPORTANT TO MASTURBATE?

A: I think the biggest thing is learning about your body and how you respond to different sexual stimuli. Masturbating by yourself is ultimately the safest place you can be sexual. Even though nobody's talking about doing it, lots of people are doing it. It is my personal belief that masturbating is really good for you and for your self-esteem—being with yourself, enjoying yourself.

Q: WHY ARE PEOPLE ASHAMED OF MASTURBATING?

A: I think that's changing, definitely more people are talking about it. I think people are ashamed of it because for a long time it was something you didn't do, it was not something talked about, and it was not taught in sex education. Also there's the fact that certain religions believe and teach that it is something to be ashamed of.

Q: DO AS MANY GIRLS MASTURBATE AS BOYS?

A: I think a lot of boys start earlier because they're not told they shouldn't masturbate. Whereas with women, it is considered something you don't really talk about. There are so many slang terms for male masturbation and so few for female masturbation. I think a lot of boys do it younger. There are lots of young women who do it too, but you will find there are some women who are in their twenties and haven't masturbated. I think with women it's a longer journey to figure out their sex and their sexuality.

Q: WHY IS IT MORE SOCIALLY ACCEPTABLE FOR BOYS TO MASTURBATE THAN FOR GIRLS?

A: I think it's because boys are not subjected to the same kind of notions about virginity and the need to be pure.

Q: IF YOU MASTURBATE WITH A DILDO DOES IT MEAN YOU ARE NOT A VIRGIN?

A: A lot of people have different views of what virginity is. I think that most people think that until you're with someone else, you're a virgin, whether you masturbate or not. Medically, if there is a hymen intact, then you are supposed to be a virgin, but the thing is a lot of people can break their hymen in non-sexual ways, like bike riding or horseback riding. Therefore, having a hymen does not define virginity. So it's kind of a vague notion and people have different ideas about what virginity is.

Q: HOW DO YOU KNOW IF YOU ARE HAVING AN ORGASM WHEN YOU ARE MASTURBATING?

A: It takes time to figure it out. That was my experience masturbating when I was young. But eventually you know. You feel an incredible body buzz and you feel it go through your body. And there are lots of different kinds of orgasms, and even if you don't have one, you can still have a good time.

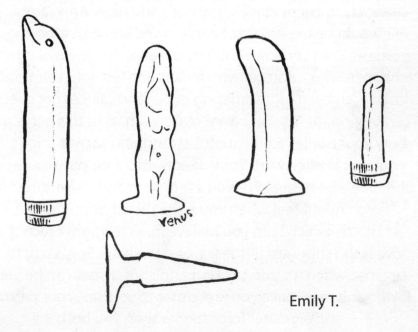

Venus

Emily T.

93

Can a body be a temple? Can sex be a prayer to something higher, greater than ourselves? Despite the impression I get from most major religions, sex can be an incredibly spiritual and soulful experience. The warm, smooth, and heated friction between bodies cannot only be beneficial to our minds and hearts, but to our souls as well.

Corrine Aberdeen

Spirituality and Sex

I feel that many religions don't give sex the spiritual credit it deserves. Too often sex is seen as a mindless or even evil act engaged in by two people who can't control themselves, or as only a means to an end – babies! But some ancient religions believed that sex was one of the ultimate channels to connect with gods or goddesses. An example of this would be the orgasm. People could argue that having an orgasm is a very powerful spiritual experience. Having this happen with a partner who makes you feel safe, calm, and loved is an even more amazing experience, since that special connection makes you aware of how amazing this act is, and how your bodies are beautiful, strong, and sacred things. As you cuddle afterwards, look deeply into your partner's eyes and take a deep breath – you'll feel calm and relaxed, just like you might feel when you say a prayer or meditate.

No matter which faith you believe in, all religions teach that love is the strongest virtue anyone can have. Sex is a natural act that, when it's safe, trusting, and consensual, can be very loving and may make you feel closer to yourself, your partner, and a greater force higher than you both.

Top 10 Questions
We Had about Sex ...

**Questions and answers compiled from
the Arcade Down & Dirty discussion group
facilitated by Jessica Harrod and Bridget Sinclair,
Youth Services Workers, St. Stephen's Community House**

In no particular order...

1) Does sex hurt, and if so, why?

Sex for girls, especially the first time, can be painful and there are a few reasons for this. If you are nervous about having sex for the first time, getting caught, etc., your muscles may tense up, resulting in your vagina being very tight. This will make it difficult for the penis to enter, and it will be uncomfortable. Also, the vagina needs lubrication for sex to be comfortable. If you are not lubricated, sex can cause friction, which is painful or irritating. SO lube up ladies! (See next question for info on lubes.)

Finally, women have this lovely little layer of tissue called the hymen that sometimes covers the vaginal opening. When the hymen is torn, it can sometimes be painful, and even bleed a little bit. The hymen can also be torn by riding a horse, inserting a tampon, masturbating ... anything really.

2) How can I make sex more pleasurable?

Firstly, most people agree that having sex with someone you care about, respect and feel respected by, and are turned are on by can really help to make sex more enjoyable.

Also, masturbating and finding out what you like is totally important to helping your partner pleasure you! Don't be afraid to tell your partner what you like and don't like ... it's sexy, so lend a helping hand!

Before you have sex, try having lots of foreplay. Make out, touch each other, get your partner to eat you out, or masturbate. This will help you relax, make you wetter and bring you closer to achieving an orgasm. While having sex, don't forget about the clit! Find a position where it's easy for your partner to touch your clit during sex (like woman on top). Most girls orgasm from clitoral stimulation, not vaginal penetration! It's all about experimentation; everyone's different, and exploring what makes you feel good with your partner and on your own is tons of fun!

Another helpful tip for girls is to USE LUBE when you are having sex. If you are using a latex condom, make sure you use water-based lube, cuz oil-based lube can make the condom break.

3) What and where are the clitoris and the G-spot?

The clitoris is a sexual organ and the only part of the human body designed purely for pleasure! So here are some quick directions on how to find it: where the lips of your vagina meet at the top (the end furthest from your bum) there's a small fold of skin, and hiding underneath is the clit. As you get aroused, the clit will swell with blood .... it's kinda like a girl's version of an erection.

The G-spot is a bit more complicated; in fact, it'll probably take a while to master it on your own, let alone with a partner. The G-spot is a mass of nerve tissue inside the vagina. Slowly insert one or two lubricated fingers into the vagina, and using your index finger, make a "come here" motion with your fingers. Some women find this incredibly exciting, but some are indifferent or don't like it at all.

SO there ya go! Find a private place where you and your partner can find your clit and G-spot together, and have fun!

4) How do you put on a condom?

Here are a few quick easy steps on how to put on a condom!
1. Store your condoms in a cool, dry place.
2. Check the packaging to make sure the condom has not expired, and carefully tear the package open ... don't bite it, the condom might rip!
3. For extra pleasure put a drop or two of water-based lube inside the condom.
4. Squeeze the tip of condom with your forefinger and thumb when rolling the condom all the way down the erect penis. This will leave space for the semen.
5. After ejaculation, withdraw the penis while holding the condom firmly in place.

6. Tie the condom in a knot so you don't spill any of the cum, and throw it out in the garbage. Do not flush it down the toilet.

5) How do you give oral sex?

Giving oral sex is all about communication ... in fact, *all* sexual activities are about communication! Telling partners what feels good is so important. Also, with any sort of oral sex you want to find a position that you're both comfortable in, considering you don't know how long you're going to be down there!

When giving oral sex to a woman, focus on the clitoris—lick it, suck it, kiss it, all that fun stuff. One technique is to spell out the alphabet with your tongue on your partner's clit!

When giving head to a guy, the main pleasure spot is around the head of the dick. Most guys don't enjoy the feeling of teeth when receiving head – to avoid this, put your lips over your teeth. Remember that you don't have to swallow his semen when he ejaculates; it's totally up to you. In fact, you don't have to have his cum in your mouth at all! Just ask him beforehand to tell you when he's going to cum, and finish him off with your hand.

Oral sex isn't for everyone. If it isn't something you enjoy doing, remember that you don't have to! There are tons of fun alternatives to oral sex.

6) What does an orgasm feel like?

An orgasm is a feeling of intense pleasure, and it's almost impossible to explain! Here are some people's attempts:
-it's an explosive, ecstatic, avalanche of sensations
-it's a rollercoaster ride
-it's like lowering into a hot bath
-it's a surge of energy
-it's like a really great sneeze

Sorry I can't explain better, and I know this sucks to hear, but you'll know when you have one!

7) If I have sex when I'm on my period, can I get pregnant?

Yes! You can get pregnant ! The only way to help prevent pregnancy is finding a birth control method that works for you. See the chapters on birth control, STIs, and HIV/AIDS for more information on how to protect yourself.

8) What counts as losing your virginity?

This is different for everyone; however, most people consider the losing of virginity the act of penetration with another person. It's up to you what you want to define as your own virginity.

9) How do girls masturbate?

Most women masturbate by rubbing, touching, stroking, etc., their clitoris. You can do this with your hands, although some women enjoy using a dildo, vibrator, pillow, or any other prop they can use to pleasure themselves. It's a good idea to find a place where you have privacy and you can relax and take your time enjoying your body.

10) What do I do if I think/know I'm pregnant?

If you think you're pregnant, you should first talk to someone you trust. You can also get a home pregnancy test or go to a clinic two weeks after the suspected impregnating act. If you go before that, the results may not be accurate.

If you are pregnant, you have three options: abortion, adoption, or motherhood. Abortion is the terminating of a pregnancy, adoption is carrying the pregnancy to term and then allowing the child to be raised by another family, and motherhood is carrying the pregnancy to term and keeping the child.

None of these decisions is going to be easy to make, and it's important to think it through and determine what will be right for you. If you are a teen and pregnant, it would probably be a good idea to find a counselor to help go through these options so you can know the facts and the details for all of them. Remember, having a child isn't the end of the world. There are tons of awesome, successful young mothers!

For more information, see Chapter Five and the resources section at the back of this book.

Birth Control

So, if you're enjoying and exploring the wonderful world of sex, perhaps you should take a closer look at this chapter: Birth Control. We lucky chicks have the wonderful ability to become impregnated. Which is great ... but ... also a huge concern when one is sexually active. This chapter explores all the various types of birth control available, as well as how to get them.

Chi Nguyen

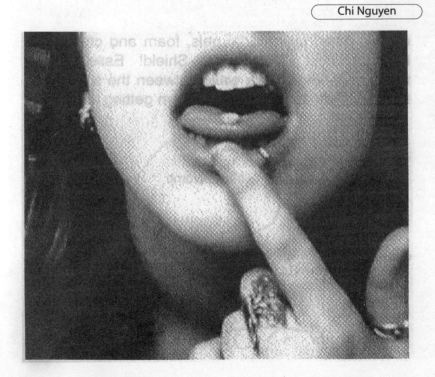

Birth Control – It's all up to YOU!

The Group

No one knows your body better than you, and if you are sexually active, you need to be aware of all the possible consequences. Besides sexually transmitted infections (STIs), sexually active women must also be aware of the possibility of pregnancy.

As a sexually active female, it is important to have the knowledge necessary to make wise decisions for yourself and your future, and if at that moment a child is not part of the equation, there are countless methods to prevent pregnancy. Most birth control methods can be purchased without a prescription, but with so many options (from patches to pills), it all comes down to you.

No one knows you better than yourself, and while some of these methods might seem foolproof, there are some side effects to be aware of. For example, the Pill, an oral contraceptive (which is a dose of hormones—usually estrogen and/or progesterone) *sometimes* has side effects that can suck (like irregular menstrual bleeding, nausea, weight gain, headaches, dizziness, breast tenderness, and mood changes). In women over 35 and smokers, the likelihood while on the Pill of heart attack, stroke, and blood clots is greatly heightened. While this may seem quite scary, every women is unique, and while some may experience side effects, many do not.

Birth Control

Sarah Lawrences

the ins and outs ...

So, I went to this clinic to learn about birth control. It was kinda cool. The woman took me into this little room that had comfy couches and pictures of ovaries on the walls. She had this large plastic container that held the keys to my questions.

She asked me what I knew about birth control and I decided to play dumb. I wanted to get the full spiel from her.

She told me that there are two types of birth control:

Barrier Methods

First she talked about "barrier methods." These include condoms, diaphragms, female condoms, and let's not forget about the Lea Shield! Essentially, all these methods are like walls between the sperm and the cervix. Each should be used with spermicidal gel, foam, and/or cream for maximum protection against pregnancy.

Condoms are the number one invention of all time! Condoms are probably the best form of contraceptives out there for us young gals. Not only do they protect you from pregnancy but also from STIs — BUT you gotta learn to use them properly. They are 85% to 98% effective; condoms with a spermicide are most effective. Many condoms are made of latex (but there are many other kinds), which is a thin plastic-like material. You slide the condom over the penis before you have sex and it catches all the cum when he ejaculates.

A **diaphram** is a shallow cup made of rubber, shaped like a dome. You have to be fitted by a doctor and it can be reused for up to a year. It's made of soft material so that you can fold it and place it up inside your vagina. You need to be refitted if you have an abortion, get pregnant, or gain or lose weight of 4.5 kg (10 lbs) or more. The diaphragm can be used while you are on your period. You put it in with spermicidal jelly and bonk away. Six hours after the bonking is done, you remove it.

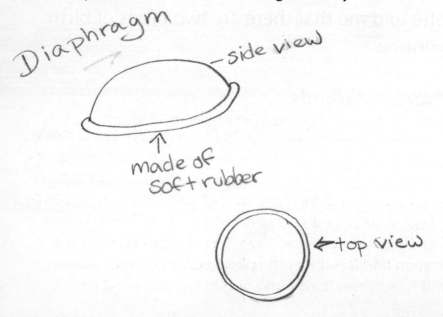

Diaphragm — side view

↑ made of soft rubber

← top view

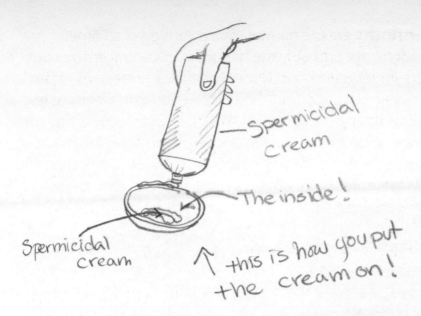

Spermicidal cream

The inside!

Spermicidal cream

↑ this is how you put the cream on!

You have to squirt more gel up your vagina periodically. Oh, and you have to use a condom with it to help protect you from those nasty STIs and HIV!

To use a diaphram, you have to be very comfortable touching your vagina. I thought about my friends using it. There are a few that would, but on the whole it seems like something suited for older women who have had some time to get used to tampons without applicators and the like.

The **female condom** is a long plastic baggy that is made of polyurethane or plastic. It has a ring at the top and at the bottom. You insert the closed side in and it sits up against your cervix, like a diaphragm, while the other ring sits outside of your vagina. Apparently it can be rather noisy while you are having sex. It lies over top of your clitoris; some women find it reduces the pleasure, while other women find it increases it, with the ring being there and all.

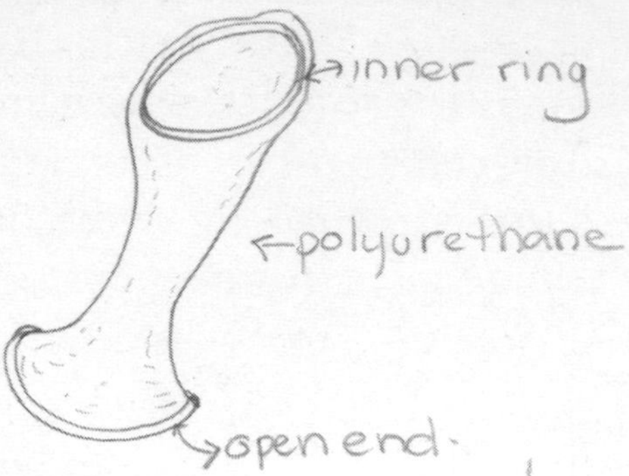

inner ring

←polyurethane

open end

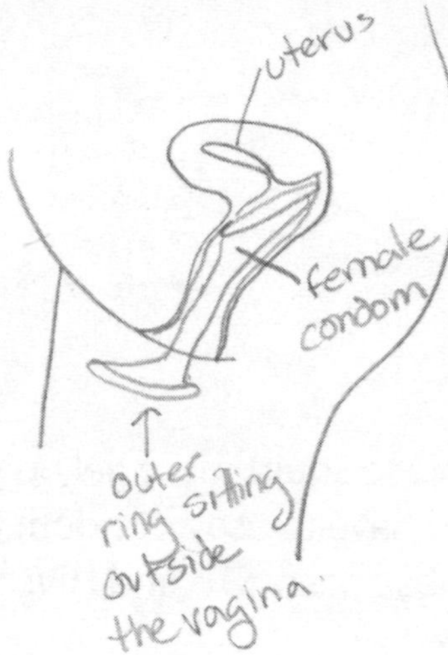

uterus

female condom

Outer ring sitting outside the vagina

Next is **Lea's shield**. This is the most bizarre thing I have ever seen. It looks kinda like the space ship *Enterprise*, from Star Trek. It was designed by this guy and he named it after his wife LEA. (I thinks that's really funny!) It goes up inside your vagina against your cervix and it blocks the sperm, BUT it has this valve that allows some vaginal fluid to be released, which helps with the lubrication. Pretty cool, eh? You need to use spermicide with it and keep it in six to eight hours after sex. In Canada, this is something you can buy in a drug store. In the US, you need a prescription. Lea's shield is made of silicone and it lasts for a long time, but you have to be super comfortable with touching yourself and sticking objects up your vagina!

OK so then there are the various **spermicides**—creams, gels, films, and foams. These all work to prevent sperm from getting to your eggs by killing the sperm before it reaches your cervix. You use them with other barrier methods, especially condoms or a diaphragm, for extra protection. Some women have uncomfortable reactions to the chemicals in spermicidal gel and foams; film can be less irritating. Spermicides should not be confused with lubricants such as K-Y or Astroglide. Lubricants don't kill sperm; they help make a condom safer (as long as they are water-based!) and more pleasurable by making sure everything is slippery enough and won't tear as easily.

Non-Barrier Methods

After the woman at the clinic showed me all the barrier methods, she took out all these little packages of pills. Some packages of **hormones** were round, others square.

The Pill is something most of us have heard about. There are a lot of pros and cons when it comes to the Pill and it's a really personal decision. How the Pill works is that you take it every day at the same time and it tricks your body, with hormones, so that you don't ovulate (see Chapter 2 for more information). When you have sex, there is no egg to fertilize so you can't get preggers! If you forget a Pill you have to take it right

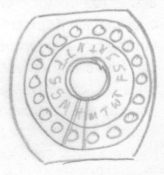

away or double up the next day and use condoms for sure for the rest of the month. Some women don't use condoms when they are taking the Pill and so are putting themselves at risk for STIs, including HIV/AIDS.

Other drawbacks are that not everyone can take it. You shouldn't take it if you have high blood pressure or a family history of severe high blood pressure. There are potential side effects with the Pill: some women retain water, their breasts get bigger, and it can affect your skin (more or fewer acne pimples). Some women feel less interested in sex, some are more interested in sex, some have headaches. Many women don't experience any side effects.

Besides being really easy to use, the positive aspects of the Pill are: it reduces the risk of endometrial and ovarian cancer, and it makes your period shorter and less painful.

To get the Pill, you need to make an appointment to see a doctor. The doctor will check your blood pressure and review your family history. It's a good idea to have an internal exam and a breast exam either before you start the Pill or within the first three months, especially if you're sexually active. The doctor may ask you to return in three months to check to see if you are OK and to check your blood pressure. Sometimes you have to try different types of Pills before you find one that works for you. If you find the Pill you are on is causing bad side effects, you can be switched to another type. You have to be patient.

Nuva Ring is a flexible contraceptive ring that is made of vinyl acetate and magnesium sterarate. It is about five centimeters (two inches) in diameter and is used to prevent pregnancy. You insert it into your vagina just once a month. The muscles in your vagina wall will keep it in place for three weeks. During this time, it will slowly release a low dose of the hormones estrogen and progesterone that prevent pregnancy. When 21 days are completed, remove Nuva Ring to let your body have its menstrual cycle (period), and after 7 days, you put in a new ring. You need to use a condom with this one too 'cause it doesn't protect against STIs and HIV/AIDS.

Ortho Evra, better known as "the patch", releases a steady dose of estrogen and progestin hormones that prevent pregnancy. A new patch is worn every week (in a different spot each week) for three weeks. The patch is 4 cm x 4 cm (1.5 in. x 1.5 in.), beige or brown, and can be applied to the lower abdomen, buttocks, upper back, or outside upper arms, but not to the breasts. The skin must be healthy and clean of lotion, perfume, make-up, and powder. The patch is extremely sticky and will stay on your body even if you shower, sweat, swim, or go to a sauna. Your first patch should be applied on the first day of your period – if you apply it 24 hours after, you won't be protected against pregnancy for the next week. During the fourth week, you don't wear the patch. This is the week you'll have your period. Some women may feel sore breasts and/or itchy skin around the patch. The patch is just as effective as the Pill, and has a 98% stick-on rate. Remember those condoms! No STI or HIV/AIDS protection here either.

I had also heard about something called **Depo-Provera**, so I asked the woman about it. Yikes! Good thing I did. Depo-Provera is a long-acting progestin (hormone) form of birth control. It is injected into the deltoid muscle (in your arm) every 11 weeks. It starts being effective 24 hours after your first injection if given in the first 5 days of a normal menstrual period. You will need to receive your injection promptly every 11 weeks in order to continue your contraceptive protection. The woman said Health Canada had issued an official warning against Depo-Provera due to research that shows it may cause irreversable loss of bone mass density and can contribute to osteoporosis. Doctors were encouraged not to give D-P to teens.

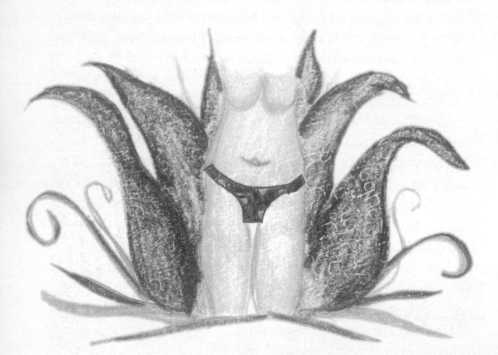

You gotta have a
Plan B
Emergency Contraceptive Pill

What do you do if, in the heat of the moment, you don't use a condom? Or you forget to take the Pill? Or you are sexually assaulted and think you might get pregnant? Plan B is an emergency contraceptive that can be taken within 72 hours of when you had sex.

Plan B is available over the counter in Canada and in some US states. It is 89% effective when taken properly. You will get two tablets. The first one is taken orally as soon as possible within 72 hours of unprotected sex. The second one can be taken at the same time or up to 12 hours after the first. The sooner they're taken, the more effective they are. The pills are *not* effective if you are already pregnant; they prevent fertilization and implantation, but don't terminate a pregnancy. They also do nothing in terms of protecting you from STIs.

Other stuff to know about Plan B:

* Plan B can be taken up to five days after sex, but its effectiveness drops to only 58%!!!

* Side effects may include nausea and your next period coming early.

* If you throw up within one hour of taking either pill, talk to your pharmacist or doctor about getting another pill.

Imogen Birchard

AAHH ... The Joy and Bliss of Latex Allergies

Uh oh ... all this talk of latex condoms, but what if when you use one you get a rash, it burns, it's red and itchy on your genitals? Sounds like you've got a latex allergy. But have no fear! There's an awesome alternative. There's POLYURETHANE condoms. Polyurethane is the stuff that the female condoms are made of, and now some male condoms as well! Some brands to check out are Durex Avanti (the most widely available brand of polyurethane condoms) and Trojan Supra. Polyurethane condoms are as effective as latex, BUT they're more likely to break ... so make sure you follow the directions on the package. They also conduct body heat better so they feel thinner than they really are, and this makes sex more pleasurable. Polyurethane condoms help protect from STIs and HIV/AIDS as well as pregnancy, so all in all they're just as good as latex! However, they are more expensive than latex, but you can get them at any drug store.

If you think you have a latex allergy, you should go to your doctor to figure out what else might help. You might be allergic to the spermicide on the condom, not the latex itself, so try non-spermicidal condoms. It will just take some research!

Imogene Birchard

The Pill

I went on the Pill when I was 13 years old. I had gone to a health clinic and they thought it would help with my periods. My periods were 10 days long and very painful.

When I was 15 years old, I started dating Mark. He was older and cute, and we laughed a lot about really silly things. We would sit in his room and play rummy 500 endlessly. We laughed all the time.

I decided I was ready to have sex. We tried several times before it actually happened. First, we tried on Algonquin Island, in broad daylight. I was really uncomfortable and it hurt like hell. He couldn't get it in, so we gave up. I was bruised for days.

We tried again in his bedroom. I was not really interested but I felt I had to. Again, it was unsuccessful and hurt like hell. I cried this time and we gave up.

Finally, in the laundry room, it worked. I was not thrilled. It was awkward and painful. I decided to stay on the Pill since I was having sex. I didn't think about STIs or AIDS. I didn't connect that with me.

When I was 18 years old I started to get yeast infections. Most women will experience one or two in their lives, but I had a yeast infection for a full year! I tried all the remedies: yogurt tampons, cranberry juice, no sugar, no caffeine, and cotton undies. I read all the books, talked to a million women about their experiences ... I did everything. Finally, I was given medicine.

Let's picture what your arm might look like if you had an allergic reaction to cream. Now imagine what your vagina would look like with an allergic reaction to cream. That was me, in bed

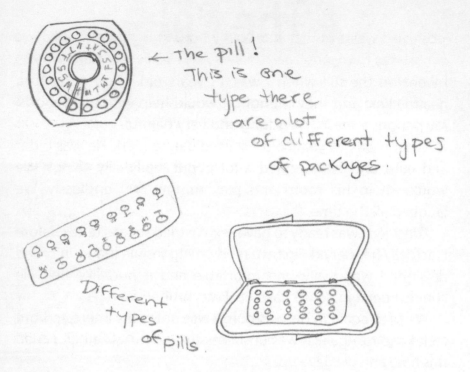

← The pill!
This is one
type there
are a lot
of different types
of packages.

Different
types
of pills.

for two weeks straight, not able to walk or anything. I was totally embarrassed and in pain.

At this point, the doctor suggested I be tested for HIV. I had had one other boyfriend since Mark. I had never used a condom and I knew Mark had fooled around behind my back. When the doctor told me that chronic yeast infections could be a symptom of AIDS, I felt numb all over. I left her office and went straight to my mom's. I wasn't even going to tell my mom, but when I saw her, I broke down in tears. I was so scared.

I had the test and it took three long, miserable, bloody weeks. When I went back to her office for the results, I was ready to barf, I was so scared. I thought it would make sense for me to be HIV positive. I was this nice little girl who had been with only two boys; I was from a normal family. It had *People Magazine* written all over it.

I wanted to hug the doctor when she said the test was negative! I went out and celebrated in a big way with everyone. But why was I still getting yeast infections?

Finally, my doctor suggested I go off the Pill. So after seven years of taking it, I said good-bye to the Pill.

It was a miracle: within a month I was fine! I was so happy, BUT at the same time I was pissed off. I went out to learn more about this bloody Pill. What I learned I was not thrilled with.

I realized that there are a lot of positives about the Pill, BUT there are negatives for some women. I wasn't given all the information. It turned out that some women get yeast infections while on the Pill. I have since spoken to people at Public Health and at various clinics, and some people say it is rare for yeast infections to be a side effect, but I have known a couple of women who have experienced it.

I guess what I am saying is get the facts about any medication!!! Always wear a condom and if birth control is your priority then also try the Pill and see how it works for you. Give it three months, and if it is not working, then try something else (see earlier in this chapter for other options). The key thing I discovered in all of this is that you have to learn about what you put in your body before you take it. From now on, I will read and ask questions and I will demand that people working in the medical field give patients all the information before they push them to make a decision.

Anonymous

My Choice

Penny Nicholls

My intention wasn't to choose a birth control that day, let alone start trying one out, but it was that easy. I went to a birth control clinic with a friend of mine who was getting her Pap test. While waiting, I talked to a women about my birth control options. There were many, but she focused on two: the Pill and a new form of birth control called Ortho Evra, better known as the patch.

I knew a little about the Pill previously and wasn't sure it was for me because I worried about having to remember to take them daily, as well as the fact I have a problem swallowing things like Tylenol. I hadn't heard of the patch, but when she told me about it, I was really interested because it covered both my concerns about the Pill.

See, you put a sticker-like patch on your lower abdomen, buttocks, upper back, or your upper arm and leave it there for a whole week. The patch slowly releases hormones into your body that help prevent pregnancy. Unlike the Pill, there is an extra amount of hormones (two days' worth) so if you forget to change it on your regular change day, you have two days to do so.

All of what I heard seemed safe, convenient, and really easy so I told her I was interested in trying the patch out. I assumed I'd have to come back and pick up a prescription, but she informed me I could have a free starter kit, which included one month's worth of the patches, a case, and an information booklet. So, I applied the patch to what I thought to be the most concealed spot of my body options, my lower abdomen.

I've been on the patch for about six months now, and unfortunately, I've started to endure some side effects that have me contemplating switching the form I use. Keep in mind, not all girls endure the same or all of the reported possible side effects; it differs for each girl's body. The first months were fine, no differences, except from some breast growth and tenderness, which didn't really have me complaining. Oh and sometimes clothing fuzz would stick to my skin around the patch, but it's easy to remove with baby oil. However, around month four I started to have mood swings; at first they were rare and little but now they've got me thinking I'm crazy sometimes. It's not all the time, but it still bothers me, so I'm looking into other options I have for birth control.

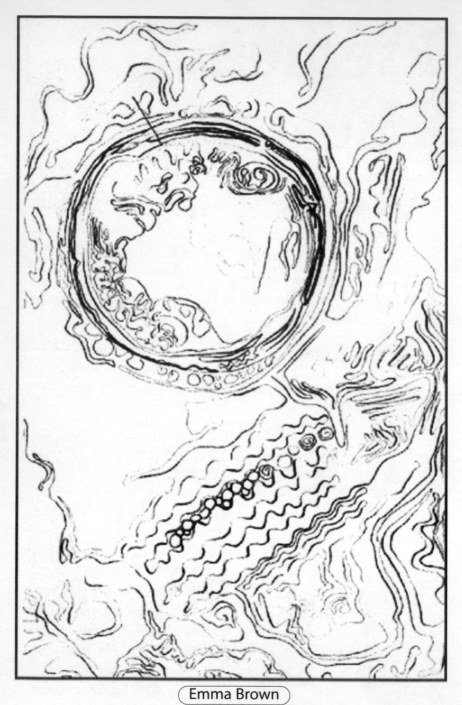

Emma Brown

Pregnancy/ Miscarriage

Chapter 5

Imogen Birchard and Andrew Coinbra

WOW. The general fear among sexually active girls ... PREGNANCY. Each and every time, we worry worry worry, but some of us still take the same risks again and again. Teenage pregnancy is a complicated issue. Choosing to give life at any age is a huge huge huge commitment. Choosing to bring a child into the world as a teenager is an even bigger one. There is some crucial information about pregnancy in the interviews in this chapter. Read on for some very intense stories about teenage pregnancy and miscarriages.

Chi Nguyen

My Choice

Waiting for the results,
My patience grew thin,
I knew we should have used a condom,
Now there's no way to win.

Just as I thought,
My suspicions were true,
Now comes the decision,
Of what I should do.

The day will soon come,
For this young teen,
When the baby inside,
Can plainly be seen.

Do I keep my baby,
Whose father's not here,
To raise on my own,
Despite my own fear?

I could carry to term,
And give it away,
For some family to raise,
But at what price to pay?

If I choose abortion,
What will society say?
But if it's right for me,
It's the only way.

Confused am I,
As to what I should do,
I want what's best,
It's all too new.

Whatever I choose,
It's my choice alone,
Not for others,
To condemn or condone.

Joy Stewart

Jessica Johnston

Pregnancy Interview

Interview by Hilary Quigley with Denah Smith, B.Sc.N., Registered Nurse

Q. What are some ways of NOT getting pregnant?
A. The best way to be sure to not get pregnant would be to not have intercourse. There are many pleasurable sexual activities that couples can enjoy without the risk of pregnancy. If you ARE having intercourse, make sure to use a birth control method—such as the Pill or a vaginal contraceptive, such as a diaphragm or vaginal foam as well as a lubricated latex condom—to help prevent pregnancy.

Choosing to engage in sexual activity carries with it a lot of responsibility and there are consequences to these actions, not only physically, but mentally and emotionally as well. It is always best to gain as much information as possible before making these choices.

Q. What role do drugs play in getting pregnant?
A. When you are drunk or high, your ability to think straight is altered. Your judgment is not always clear and you may get caught up in the moment and not think ahead to how important it is to insist on using condoms and birth control. Young women can also be at greater risk of being sexually assaulted when they are high or drunk. Often couples forget about using birth control and put themselves at risk for pregnancy or STIs. You might also have sex with someone that you wouldn't have if you had been sober.

Q. How can you find out if you're pregnant or not?
A. You may feel tired, have sore breasts, or experience frequent peeing or vomiting. But the only way to know for sure if you are pregnant is to take a pregnancy test when your period is late. You can do a home pregnancy test or be tested by your doctor or at a clinic. Home pregnancy test kits are able to detect a hormone in your pee that confirms whether you are pregnant or not; these can be used as early as a week after a missed period. Results are confirmed within minutes. Your doctor or a clinician at a clinic can do a blood or urine test to confirm

119

the pregnancy. (See resource guide at the back of this book for information on how to find places to be tested).

Q. Is a condom 100% safe?
A. A condom is 97% safe as protection against STIs (like HIV) and pregnancy as long as it doesn't break, leak, or fall off, and as long as it's used consistently. KEEP IN MIND, condoms do not protect you from all sexually transmitted diseases—such as genital warts. You can never expect a condom to always protect you or your partner, therefore it is also recommended to use condoms that are lubricated with spermicidal (sperm-killing) gel to increase protection.

Put the condom on before the penis touches the vagina. Men leak fluids from their penises before and after ejaculation. Pre-ejaculate ("pre-cum") can carry enough sperm to cause pregnancy. It can also carry enough germs to pass sexually transmitted infections. Use a condom only once. Use a fresh one for each erection ("hard-on"). Have a good supply of condoms on hand.

Condoms usually come rolled into a ring shape. They are individually sealed in aluminum foil or plastic. Be careful — don't tear the condom while unwrapping it. If it is torn, brittle, stiff, or sticky, throw it away and use another.

Q. Is there a higher risk of a girl getting pregnant when she is on her period?
A. A lot of young women think they can't get pregnant if they are on their period. It is less likely that she will get pregnant, but new ovulation can begin before the end of your period, so it is possible to get pregnant.

Q. How can recreational drugs affect your pregnancy?
A. If you do things like smoke weed/pot/marijuana/hash or drink alcohol, it could hurt the baby. Drugs and alcohol are passed on to the baby when you are pregnant. It is very dangerous! If you smoke cigarettes while you are pregnant, it raises the baby's heart rate and can result in low birth weight, which can result in further health problems for your baby. And even one drink of alcohol can increase the possibility of irreversible birth defects from fetal alcohol syndrome (FAS).

Q. How does having a baby as a teen affect your friends and family?

A. It can have a huge effect on friends and family. If you are responsible for your child, your life will change drastically. Whether you continue school or work, there are many childcare issues and costs. Your social life will change. Babysitters will be required and they are not cheap. Often families are angry and may ask the mother to leave the house. There are also some families that work together to raise the child. There are many emotional and financial issues, not to mention the long term effects, such as employment later on in life. A lot of young mothers haven't finished growing up and developing as people themselves and they need help with parenting skills.

Q. Why do teens get pregnant?

A. There are many reasons why teens get pregnant. They may not have the knowledge, money, or access to birth control information that they need. They may not be able to use birth control for religious reasons. They may be having unprotected sex to please their partner or to rebel against their parents. Often it is an accident—the condom broke, they forgot to take their Pill, or they may have been raped.

Q. If a young mother decides to put her child up for adoption, how can she stay in touch with her child?

A. Usually when a mother gives her child up for adoption, she will not know who the adoptive parents are and they won't know her either. In an "open adoption," the birth parents and adoptive parents agree on periodic contact—where they can arrange times to meet and visit. If it is a "semi-adoption," then the birth mother would be allowed special visitation rights and would be allowed to send cards and letters and make phone calls. Otherwise the birth mother is not allowed to contact the child. When the child gets older, the child can try to contact the birth parents.

Q. What role should the father play in all of this?

A. The father of the child should be around to support with money, comfort, and love. He should not leave all the work up to the mother. He should be there and have equal responsibility with the mother. Often the father does not take part in all this. The court may order him to contribute financially to the child. Sometimes the situation is very complicated (for example, in the case of rape, or unknown father) and having the father involved is not possible.

Ready or not?

It really irritates me when adults say things like, "If you are not mature enough to take proper precautions about sex, then you are not mature enough to have sex at all." Most of us already know that the number one rule is that you always have to use an effective form of protection against STIs and pregnancy. The reality of life though, is that it doesn't always happen that way.

I know five people who got pregnant around the age when I started having sex, that being 15. Two have had abortions. Of the three who decided to keep the baby, one is currently pregnant, and another had an awful miscarriage. Some people would say that the miscarriage was a blessing in disguise, but to my friend it was really tragic. My friend that carried her baby to term is doing fine, a happy ending you don't often hear with teen pregnancy stories. She is a level-headed woman who knew what she was getting herself into. As for my friends who had the abortions, I am really proud of them for knowing what they could and couldn't handle. That they knew what they had to do is just as responsible as my friend who kept her child. One choice is not more responsible or smarter than the other. I respect them both equally.

A lot of adults don't understand that many pregnant young women are just as capable as any adult to have a kid. Some young women aren't, I know, but most of the ones that aren't know that they aren't ready for the lifetime commitment of a baby. Young women are a lot smarter than a lot of people make them out to be.

Maybe more teens need to give each other lectures about how to have safe sex and about the dangers of unprotected sex. As far as I'm concerned though, birth control is completely up to me. If I want to take precautions, that is my prerogative, but if I don't, I do not want to be made to feel bad for making a decision I thought a lot about and felt was right for me.

If you're thinking about having sex, just make sure you know all your options, and that you're ready in your mind and body.

Anonyomous, 17

It's amazing how we can create a real human body inside of our very own body. It's incredible how we push an infant out of our bodies and have that baby have the same body and facial features as us.

But what's even more incredible is that you and I can wait until we are older, more experienced, more mature, and more developed (mentally and physically) to give birth to a child.

Because if we're going to bring a human being into this world, we better do it right!!!!!

Suvi Siu, age 15

STRENGTH~ BEAUTY ~ SPIRIT

STRENGTH

Suvi Siu

Untitled
I never needed your love
Like I do now
I know you don't care
But you'll learn to, somehow ...

I never needed your support
Like I do now
Back me up my friend
And I'll learn to somehow ...

I never needed your friendship
Like I do now
Be my friend
And together, we'll learn how ...

REGAN

124

Pregnant and Alone

KARREEN, age 16

Why can't I breathe when I hear of the topic? Is it just me?

Or does the whole world understand?

I am a child in the universe and I am alone with no one and nothing!

What should I do?

Where should I go, and who should I blame?

Can I take it all myself?

PREGNANCY!!!

Is this word everywhere?

I am pregnant with me and by myself, nobody knows and nobody cares.

I feel ashamed and confused ...

I'm still young in a big world and with myself and my child.

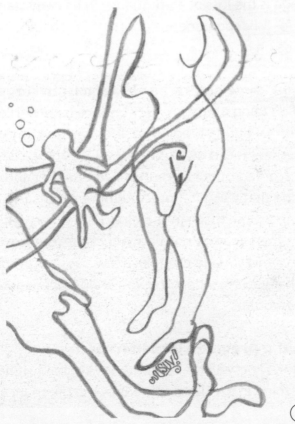

Suvi Siu

125

Miscarriage Interview

Interview by Hilary Quigley
with Denah Smith, B.Sc.N., Registered Nurse

Q. What is a miscarriage?

A. A miscarriage is the loss of a pregnancy in its early stages. The medical term for it is "spontaneous abortion," meaning that the pregnancy ends on its own.

Q. How do you know you're having a miscarriage?

A. Often the first thing a woman might notice is some bleeding. That can be normal during pregnancy and may go away on its own, but sometimes it can be a sign that a miscarriage is starting. If it is a miscarriage, the bleeding will get heavier and there will be cramping that will get more and more severe. There will be clots and then some tissue in the blood. If it is very early in the pregnancy, there may be nothing you can recognize.

Sometimes a miscarriage can take a few days to complete. It is important that you see a doctor if you are pregnant and have any of these symptoms.

Q. Why would a pregnancy miscarry?

A. We really don't know all the reasons why. Probably it happens because something in the development of the pregnancy didn't happen quite right. Everything has to work really beautifully in the pregnancy. If one little step doesn't work right, then a miscarriage happens. It's sort of nature's way of saying, "Well, this one didn't work out."

Q. What are some statistics on miscarriages?

A. From 15% to 20% of pregnancies will end in a miscarriage — that's one out of six. Most miscarriages occur by the time the woman reaches 12 to 13 weeks of pregnancy — that's during the first three months. Later than that is rare.

Q. Why is it called a miscarriage?

A. 'Mis' means "to do improperly", like mistake. So it means that there is a problem with the carrying of the pregnancy.

Q. Are there different kinds of miscarriages?

A. Yes, and there are different terms for different kinds of miscarriages. Some women have a "spontaneous abortion." That means everything comes out all at once. Sometimes, the process goes on for quite a while. That's called an "incomplete spontaneous abortion."

There is a third kind, called a "missed abortion." It's a miscarriage that's happened but hasn't fully come away from the uterus yet — the woman has only bled a little. Sometimes, the miscarriage will continue on its own, but sometimes the woman may need to be treated. The woman will have a "D and C," otherwise known as dilation and curettage, which is a medical procedure where the pregnancy tissue is removed. Alternatively, she will receive a drug called "misoprostol" to help the miscarriage continue.

These miscarriages are different from the kind of abortion that is done by choice. That is called a "therapeutic" or "induced" abortion.

Q. Can you make yourself have a miscarriage?
A. That would be an abortion. There have been a lot of folk remedies over the years, but it's very unsafe to do it on your own. It would be my hope that, if anybody thought they wanted to bring a miscarriage on, they would go to an abortion clinic to have it done safely.

Q. Can a miscarriage be fatal or a health risk?
A. People have bled to death or developed infections as a result of miscarriage, but in Canada and the US we have good health care so that is very, very rare. If you have a miscarriage, it's important to see a doctor.

Q. What do you do if you're having a miscarriage?
A. It depends on how far along and how bad your symptoms are. If the bleeding is really heavy or the cramping is really severe, go to the hospital emergency room so that a health professional can check you over. You can also be given something for pain if needed. Some women who know that they are going to miscarry will stay at home because they are more comfortable there. They keep in contact with their doctor and watch that their bleeding doesn't get too bad.

Q. Are there any long-term effects of miscarriages?
A. No. Miscarriages are very common. The rare woman may have miscarriages over and over. There are some medical reasons for that happening. Most women who have one miscarriage won't have another one.

Abortion

Chapter 6

Here's a topic that creates quite the debate.
It's a touchy subject for a lot of people because
of a whole bunch of morality issues. So, I'm not
going to preach or rant or whatever, because
everyone is definitely entitled to their own
opinions. I'm just going to say that abortion
is a choice that every woman is entitled to.
Enjoy the chapter.   Chi Nguyen

When I was 14, I met this guy. We dated for five

months and then we decided we were ready to have sex. I thought meeting him was the best thing that had ever happened and that the fact that I had met him would change my life forever. I was right, in a way; meeting him did change my life and having sex with him changed my life forever.

We had it all planned. Friday night, his parents went to their cottage and we went to his house. We smoked a joint to settle us down, then we watched a movie. Then we started to kiss and then we moved into his bedroom. We got to that point, the point we had never gotten to, new territory. I was scared but totally excited. He kept asking if I was OK with it all—he was great. Well, finally we did it and it was ... OK. I guess I expected rainbows and a cloud bursting, even though I knew better.

One of the problems was that the condom was hard to put on and it kinda fell off, but I was sure that was fine. I mean, we were both virgins so what else did we need to worry about? Nothin' right?! WRONG!

Three weeks later, I threw up in the morning. I felt like shit. I had no idea what was wrong. At school, I felt fine but not normal. I have this friend, Alison. She's the best and we usually get our periods around the same time. Mine is sometimes a little more irregular but as my mom says, "It's normal for a girl your age to have irregular menstrual cycles." (Why can't she say period instead of menstrual cycle?!) So Alison and I get our periods around the same time and, well, she'd had hers a week ago and I still hadn't had mine!

Alison knew I had just had sex; she was a pro in that department. So I asked her if maybe she thought I could be pregnant. We laughed, I guess partly 'cause it made us nervous and partly 'cause it would be just my luck to get pregnant the first time I had sex!!! But you know, I still didn't believe I could be, I just thought it was the flu.

Alison took me to this clinic she goes to get the Pill. It was okay, lots of young people. I was so worried I would see someone I knew. The nurse got me to pee in a cup and then I had to wait for what seemed like hours. The thing was that I still thought there was no way I would be pregnant, no way, no way. Well, you can imagine how shocked I was when the nurse came in and sat down with that sad supportive smile they all have and said I was pregnant.

OK, so life's over, end of the world, cannot tell anyone, might as well die right now!!!!

The nurse told me all this shit about my "options." I wasn't really listening. All I could think was: "I am never having sex again." When I left, they suggested I come back in a day or two to discuss my "options." I went home and lay on my bed and just stared into space, blanked out big time.

The next day, I figured I had to tell my stupid sperm-carrying boyfriend. He was pretty cool about it all, suddenly Mr. Adult. He said he would come to the clinic with me after school.

131

This time when the nurse at the clinic talked about options, I was listening. I guess what I figured out was I had two options: **1.** Have the baby, be disowned by my mother, quit school, have this child depend on me forever, never go out again ... life over. **2.** Have an abortion, kill a baby, and feel like a murderer for the rest of my life. Great options. Thanx everyone!!!

I think the nurse could see my stress; she asked my sperm-carrying boyfriend to leave us alone for a bit. Then she explained a lot of stuff.

We went over the having-a-child option: reviewed the costs involved, the places I could live, and where I could go to school. Then she explained abortions to me. She told me it wasn't a baby but an embryo and that at this point it was just a mass of tissue. She explained the procedure and how I might feel and then she started to talk about choice and that it is important that I have the "choice." I was learning that "options" and "choice" were two words these people liked a whole lot.

I went away to think again for a day or two. My boyfriend wasn't a whole lot of help. He didn't want to sway me one way or the other, but he also didn't really want to be involved.

I thought and thought and thought and thought some more. In the end I had an abortion. It changed my life forever. I realize now, two years later, it was the right decision, but it still sucks. I will always wonder what would my child have been like? Would it be a boy or girl? Would it have my brown curly hair or his red straight hair? The thing was, we broke up a few weeks after. We would never have lasted as a couple. I was happy in a way because it supported my decision. I also made the basketball team last year, which would not have happened if I were a mom.

I don't know. It was the hardest decision I had made at 14. Maybe I should have spent more time thinking about the sex that got me to that point. I guess I screwed up, but at least I had a "choice" (there's that word again) about what to do. If I could do it all again, what would I do? I don't know. I'd never agreed with abortion before, nor does my family, but in the end it made sense. I wish it were easier so I could give other girls real advice, but it's not. It's a really personal, intense thing, and like I said earlier, having the options, having the ability to choose what is right for you, is key and that goes for all sorts of areas in my life. I guess in the end, I learned a lot from this really shitty situation.

Anonymous, 16

Emily T.

Abortion Interview

Interview by Hilary Quigley
with Denah Smith, B.Sc.N., Registered Nurse

Q. What happens during an abortion?
A. The "suction abortion" is the process that uses a tube that goes into the uterus and gently sucks out the embryo. This is done in a hospital or free-standing clinic. In hospitals in Toronto, they are frequently done under a general anesthetic, so you're put to sleep to have it done. In a free standing clinic, you are given some medicine intravenously to make you kind of dopey. Then freezing is put around the cervix, the opening of the uterus. This blocks the pain. The procedure is done while you're awake but you're sedated.

There's a variation on this procedure called a "manual vacuum aspiration." This method uses something like a big syringe to provide suction. It can be done on a pregnancy up to 79 days after a woman's last menstrual period.

In Canada, abortion can be done on a pregnancy up to 20 weeks after a woman's last menstrual period. In the United States, the practice differs from area to area. Most abortion facilities will perform abortions on a pregnancy that is between 8 weeks and 12 weeks.

Q. What are the pros and cons of having an abortion?
A. The pros and cons have to do with the effect of the pregnancy and the abortion on the individual woman who is making the decision. Sometimes someone has a health condition that means pregnancy is dangerous for her physical well-being. More often, a woman is facing issues like asking herself, "Am I able to support a child?", "Do I want a child at this time?", "Do I feel like I can be responsible for a child?", "What are my circumstances?", "How do I feel about abortion?", "What are the alternatives?". It is normal for a woman to experience a range of emotions after an abortion, such as relief, sadness, happiness, and feelings of loss. Each woman is unique.

Q. Why are some people against abortions?
A. Some people object to abortion based on their moral or religious beliefs. For many people, a pregnancy represents the possibility of human life; the idea of ending that possibility is upsetting for them. Much of this issue is shaped by how you define when a life begins. Many people who are opposed to abortion believe that life begins at the moment the egg is fertilized by the sperm. Other people believe the life doesn't come into being until later in the pregnancy, when there's a more fully formed fetus that has the potential to live on its own, or even until the birth of the baby.

Q. How does it feel physically to have an abortion?
A. It depends on if you're awake or asleep. If you have a general anesthetic, you're put to sleep and so you're not aware of what's happening. Afterwards, you might have some mild cramping, like menstrual cramps, and some bleeding, like a period. Sometimes the cramping can be more severe.

If you're awake during the procedure, the experience is a little bit different and varies from woman to woman. There will be a speculum inserted in your vagina. There will be some discomfort from the local anesthetic, a numbness similar to what you'd experience at the dentist only around your vagina, not your mouth. There is some cramping, which varies from woman to woman in intensity. Most women are given some kind of painkiller. Basically, it would be like having a very painful period in terms of discomfort. The thing to remember is that it doesn't last very long. The whole procedure doesn't last more than 10 minutes.

Q. How much does it cost?
A. In Canada, the fee varies from province to province (in Ontario, the Ontario Health Insurance Plan covers the cost in hospitals and clinics). In the United States, the average cost is around $375, but it can much higher depending on the extent of the tests and examinations required.

Q. How are you protected from protestors at abortion clinics?
A. Most places have security in place to control who is allowed inside.

Q. What does abortion tissue look like?
A. It really depends on how far along the pregnancy is. In a very early pregnancy—up to 8 weeks from the woman's last period—the embryo is so small that you wouldn't be able to see it without a microscope. At 10 or 12 weeks, you may have an embryo that could be identified with the naked eye if it were intact. From then on, the fetus will have more and more identifiably human characteristics.

Q. Is abortion killing a baby?
A. That's a good question. Abortion in Canada can only be performed in the first 20 weeks of a pregnancy, and most places in the US restrict them to even earlier. At that point, if the fetus was born, there would be no chance of it surviving. In terms of what the tissue looks like early on, an embryo has no identifiable human characteristics; you could look at it and say it's not a baby. It has the potential to grow into a living human being but it is potential rather than a real human being. It's like the difference between a seed and a tree. After 8 to 12 weeks, when an embryo becomes a fetus with more identifiably human parts, the idea of abortion can be even more difficult for people. Counseling is an important part of abortion services. It should help and support a woman in making a decision that is best for her.

To find out where to go for abortion counseling and services nearest you, check out the resource section at the back of this book.

STIs
SEXUALLY TRANSMITTED INFECTIONS

Chapter 7

Another scary potential consequence of sexual activity, STIs are diseases and infections that put young women's health at risk. In this chapter, we look at some of the different types of STIs, what you can do to avoid them, and how to treat them.

With most STIs, they are treatable and it is not the end of the world if you acquire one. But they can almost always lead to more serious problems if left untreated. Sometimes there are no symptoms at all, while sometimes they are uncomfortable, even painful.
Chi Nguyen

Emily T.

Sexually Transmitted Infections

The most important information about sexually transmitted infections is that you must talk to your partner about STIs and your health BEFORE you have sex. You can pass on an STI without ever knowing you have it, and so can your partner. Before you start a sexual relationship, it is important to have both partners tested for STIs. See your doctor or visit a clinic. See the resources section at the back of this book for information on how to find a clinic in your area.

You should be tested for STIs once a year if you or your partner have sex with other people, if you had unprotected sex, or a condom (or a dental dam, etc.) breaks. If you think you have a STI, visit a doctor or clinic RIGHT AWAY. Most STIs are curable, but if you leave them for a long time untreated, they can do permanent damage and cause serious illness. Some infections can stop you from ever being able to have children or are life-threatening.

Another reason that you should get tested for STIs is because most people don't have any signs (that you would notice) of the STI but can still pass it on to someone!!

It is very important that you tell your partner about any STIs that you may have because they have a big chance of catching it!!!! If you get treated and your partner doesn't, they will just give it back to you!!!

The group

138

Questions We Had About Sexually Transmitted Infections (STIs)...

Questions and answers compiled from
the Arcade Down & Dirty discussion group
facilitated by Jessica Harrod and Bridget Sinclair,
Youth Services Workers, St. Stephen's Community House

Q. WHAT IS AN STI?
A. An STI is a sexually transmitted infection. Another term that we use for this is sexually transmitted disease (STD).

Q. HOW DO YOU GET AN STI?
A. You can get an STI through some form of sexual contact. This means sexual contact—through penis/vagina, penis/mouth, penis/anus, anus/mouth, or vagina/mouth contact.

Q. WHO CAN GET AN STI?
A. Anyone who is sexually active can get an STI. You're more likely to be at risk if you are engaging in sexual activity without protection, such as a condom.

Q. ARE ALL STIs DANGEROUS?
A. It depends on the particular infection and your definition of "dangerous." Many STIs are treatable with medication and are not life-threatening. HIV is the STI that causes AIDS, which is life-threatening. Always take precautions and practice safe sex, which will reduce your risk of contacting any STIs.

Q. WHAT ARE THE TYPES OF STIs THAT ARE MOST DAMAGING TO YOUR BODY?

A. HIV and hepatitis B, untreated gonorrhea, chlamydia, and syphilis are the most damaging STIs. HIV, hepatitis B, and human papilloma virus (HPV) have lifetime effects. (See STI descriptions later in this chapter.) Most STIs are treatable with medications.

Q. WHAT ARE SOME OF THE MOST COMMON STIs?

A. The most common STIs include herpes, gonorrhea, chlamydia and syphilis. Other common STIs are: trichomoniasis, hepatitis B, and human papilloma virus (HPV), which causes genital warts.

Q. HOW CAN YOU PROTECT YOURSELF FROM STIs?

A. If you are sexually active, the best way to protect yourself from getting an STI is by practicing safe sex. This means making sure you use condoms (and/or dental dams, etc.) during sexual activity. Also, going to a clinic to get tested periodically helps. You can be immunized for hepatitis B. Another way of protecting yourself from getting an STI is through abstaining from all sexual activity.

Q. HOW DO YOU TREAT AN STI?

A. Each STI is treated differently. For many cases, medications such as antibiotics can be prescribed by a doctor.

Q. ARE ANY OF THE STIs UNTREATABLE?

A. HIV (the human immunodeficiency virus that causes AIDS), genital warts, and herpes are lifetime diseases. This means that once you are infected by them, they remain with you forever. But there are medications that can treat the symptoms. (To learn more about the implications of HIV, see Chapter 8.)

Q. ARE SOME PEOPLE MORE LIKELY TO GET AN STI THAN OTHERS?

A. There are certain groups that have a higher risk of getting STIs than others. These include young people, women, and those who have multiple partners. Women are more at risk because of the way women's bodies are made. Our vaginas are moist environments that germs love. Also, because so much of our sex organs are internal, it's difficult to notice an infection.

Anyone who has sex without a condom is also more at risk of contracting an STI.

Q. DOES IT HURT TO HAVE AN STI?
A. Again, depending on the STI and how long it's left untreated, it can be painful. Some painful symptoms include discharge, blistering, or painful peeing.

Q. WHAT ARE SOME SYMPTOMS OF AN STI?
A. Different STIs manifest themselves in different ways. Sometimes you get tired, fever, blisters, sores, pain in the abdomen, pain when you pee, pain during sex, abnormal bleeding, unpleasant odors, unusual discharge (greater quantity and/or different color), or genital warts. But often there are no symptoms, especially in women!

Q. HOW DO YOU PASS ON AN STI?
A. An STI is passed through any form of sexual activity—which includes unprotected oral sex, vaginal sex, and anal sex—with a person who is already infected. You can also get them from unclean sex toys.

Q. IF YOU HAVE UNPROTECTED SEX WITH SOMEONE WHO HAS AN STI, WILL YOU GET IT THE FIRST TIME?
A. Yes. You would be lucky if you didn't. But it depends on the STI.

STIs

I didn't think that I would ever get an STI, but I was sexually active. I decided to go to the doctor and get a check-up. When the results came back, the doctor told me I had caught something. It was an STI that could be treated so I was lucky. The doctor told me that if I took the medication, the infection would go away. I did what the doctor told me to do and now I'm fine.

I didn't think that I had anything because I didn't have any signs or symptoms. I knew that my boyfriend at the time had given it to me because he was the only guy I had been with. I stopped talking to him after I told him to get himself checked. I guess I trusted him but sometimes that isn't enough.

I am thankful that I am all right. I am a lot more protective and alert. I don't want to go through this again because I might not be so lucky the next time.

Anonymous, 17

Syphilis

What is it and how do you get it?

Syphilis is a bacterial infection that left untreated can lead to serious complications or death. You can get it from oral sex, vaginal sex, or anal sex with someone who has the infection, or by sharing infected needles. The infection is passed through sores or rashes on the genitals, mouth, or skin.

How do you know if you have it?

First you get a sore that doesn't hurt. It is called a chancre. The sore will go away by itself. Three to six months later, you many get a body rash and feel like you have the flu. These symptoms can disappear without any treatment but the infection can continue to damage the brain, liver, heart, and blood vessels.

What do you do if you have it?

Go to your doctor and get a blood test done to confirm you have syphilis. Then your doctor can prescribe antibiotics. Tell your partners that you have syphilis so they can do the same.

Herpes

What is it and how do you get it?

Herpes is an infection and it causes sores around the mouth or on the genitals. You can get herpes from kissing someone who has these sores on their mouth or if your mouth comes in contact with sores in their genital area.

You can also get herpes by touching the sores of an infected person and then touching your eyes, mouth, or genitals.

*There are two types of herpes: simplex 1 and simplex 2. Type 1 usually is characterized by cold sores or fever blisters on the lips or face, and type 2 is a sore on the genital area.

How do you know if you have it?

• itching or tingling on your skin
• painful blisters full of liquid
• you will feel like you have the flu, and then blisters will form on your skin
• occasionally a lesion like a small cut may appear

The most reliable way of finding out if you have herpes is through a herpes cultures test. In this test, the doctor will collect a sample of fluid (called a viral culture) from a sore when it first appears in the blistering stage. The doctor will then send it to the lab to see if it's infected with the herpes virus. The test is very accurate but it may take a few days to process.

What do you do if you have it?

Go to your doctor. There is no cure for herpes, but there is medication that will help reduce the symptoms, which can reoccur throughout your life. You will need to eat well and get lots of rest.

Hepatitis B

What is it and how do you get it?
- It is a virus that can cause a serious infection of the liver.
- You get it by sharing blood, semen, vaginal fluid, or saliva.
- Hepatitis is passed on through sexual activity with someone who has it, sharing infected needles, and also through sharing some infected personal items like toothbrushes. A lot of people who have hepatitis B don't know that they have it, but they can still spread the virus without knowing.
- You can protect yourself from hepatitis B by getting a hepatitis B vaccine.

How do you know if you have it?
- you feel tired
- your lower tummy will hurt
- you aren't hungry often
- you often feel like throwing up
- your skin may look yellow
- your pee might be a strange color

Note: it is not unusual to have no symptoms.

What do you do if you have it?
You need to get a special blood test done by your doctor to confirm you have hepatitis. Most people can be cured. Some can't be cured, which can lead to long-term health problems.

Pubic Lice
Pubic lice (a.k.a. crabs) are small insects (rather than an infection), which attach themselves to human hairs, specifically pubic hairs. Common symptoms of crabs are itchy crotch, rash or faint bluish spot at the sight of the bite (oh yeah, forgot to mention, they bite), or tiny spots of blood on your undies. Pubic lice are passed from one person to another through direct physical contact and sometimes through contact with an infested person's sheets, towels, or clothes. A doctor can prescribe cream to get rid of them.

Trichomo..what!?

Christy Pubil, 17

When I was 16, I went to have my annual check-up at the doctor's office. My mom drove me there and back. A few days later a friend drove me home after school. When we arrived at my house my mom asked her to leave the room so that she could talk to me. I assumed that it must be something really serious. She asked me flat out if I was pregnant. I did have a boyfriend BUT I had never had sex. We hadn't even been naked together! I knew enough about sex to know that there was no way I was pregnant. I told her that it was not possible, but I could tell she didn't believe me. Apparently, the doctor had called. There was something wrong with my urine sample; she wanted to talk to me right away. I guess my mom assumed I was pregnant.

My friend offered to drive me up to the doctor's office. I had had the same doctor for years. On the way up there I started to question if there was any way I could be pregnant. I started to doubt all that I knew about sex.

When we arrived at the doctor's, she brought me into her office. I wasn't pregnant but I did have TRICHOMONIASIS! I had an STI and I hadn't even had sex yet!!!! I was so freaked out. I felt ashamed, confused, and scared. She explained that it was curable with antibiotics and that I would be fine. I told her I hadn't had sex yet. I could tell she thought I was full of shit. I still don't know why she would think I would lie about that. She said TRICH is one of the few STIs you can get from toilet seats.

When I left, I felt horrible; I hated that my mom would now want to know what was wrong and that neither she nor the doctor believed me that I had not had sex. On top of all that I had to figure out how I felt about having TRICH. I didn't want anyone to know, ever.

A couple of weeks later, a friend of mine was talking about some clinic for teens that is confidential. I decided that was what I needed. I went to check it out and never looked back. I was never going to be in that situation again, having my mother involved in my health care. What if I did start having sex and needed birth control? I needed it to be private and confidential.

It has been a couple of years since I had trichomoniasis and I still hate that I had to experience that. I swore I would never have sex but I did a year later. I always insist on condoms and that my boyfriend gets a STI check. I never want to go through that again!

Trichomoniasis

What is it and how do you get it?
This is an infection that is caused by a parasite. It can cause serious health problems. The parasite can live on wet objects for a few hours; therefore it can be spread through sex toys, wash cloths, toilet seats, and saunas. It can also be transmitted through vaginal sex with someone who has it.

How do you know if you have it?
• discharge (the pasty fluid) from your vagina is green or yellow
• discharge from your vagina smells like fish
• itching, red, sore vagina and swollen labia
• pain when you have intercourse
• pain when you pee

What do you do if you have it?
You have to go to a doctor right away for treatment. Doctors can tell from your symptoms and by a test if you have it.

Gonorrhea

What is it and how do you get it?
Gonorrhea (a.k.a. the clap) is a bacterial infection that has to be treated because it can cause serious health problems. You can get it from oral, vaginal, or anal sex with someone who has it.

How do you know if you have it?
• strange discharge from your vagina
• pain when you pee

- pain in your tummy
- pain when you have sex
- itchy, red, swollen vagina

Note: most commonly, there are no symptoms.

What do you do if you have it?

Go to your doctor and get a swab of your cervix. If you have it, they will give you antibiotics.

What is it and how do you get it?

Gardnerella is a type of bacteria that grows in small amounts in women's vaginas. If there is too much gardnerella, it can cause bacterial vaginosis (BV), which results in itching and smelly discharge. It can be passed on sexually.

How do you know if you have it?

- discharge from your vagina that is white or grey
- discharge from your vagina that smells like fish

What should you do about it?

Go to the doctor and get a prescription.

What are some tips on how to lower your chances of getting a gardnerella infection?

- do not use deodorant tampons or pads, perfumed soaps, bath oils, feminine hygiene spray
- always wipe yourself from front to back after going to the toilet
- wear cotton underwear
- avoid douching

Genital Warts or Human Papilloma Virus (HPV)

What is it and how do you get it?

There are a lot of different kinds of HPV, a few of which can cause warts in the genital area. Warts are growths on your skin that appear as hard rounded bumps. You get genital warts from direct contact with your partner's warts or an infected area during unprotected oral, vaginal, or anal sex. Like herpes, it depends where the lesions are. Sometimes using a condom doesn't cover all the lesions and doesn't stop them from spreading to you.

How do you know if you have it?

• they show as hard bumps on your skin
• they may be itchy
• you may have pain during sex
• you may bleed from your vagina or anus
• your doctor can tell you if you have them by looking at them
Note: you may not know they are there; sometimes you can't see or feel them.

What do you do if you have it?

There is no cure, but the virus often leaves the body by itself. Some types of HPV are linked to cervical cancer, so it's very important to get a pelvic exam with swabs for other STIs and a Pap smear. Ask your doctor.

Chlamydia

What is it and how do you get it?

Chlamydia is caused by bacteria and is very common. If is often found in teenagers and needs to be treated. If it is not treated, it can cause serious health problems. You can get chlamydia when you have oral, vaginal, or anal sex with someone who has it.

How do you know if you have it?

- discharge from your vagina
- sometimes you will bleed a bit, even when you aren't on your period
- bleeding when you have sex
- pain when you pee
- pain when you have sex
- pain in your tummy or lower back

Note: sometimes there are no symptoms.

What do you do if you have it?

You have to go to a doctor!! Chlamydia can lead to very serious health problems in the future. Some women become infertile, meaning they can't have babies. The doctor will give you antibiotics that will make the infection go away.

Lying on My Back

I was having my STI internal check. I was lying on my back, my legs spread as my doctor was getting the cells from inside my cervix for testing. She had just finished the first two swabs (that I couldn't feel at all). Then she did the final and most painful swab, the chlamydia swab.

She uses this uncomfortable toothbrush to scrape the inside of my cervix for some cells to test for chlamydia. It hurt and the doctor said I would probably experience some spotting later on.

Finally, the swabs were finished. My legs were closed and I was free of the speculum. My doctor was talking to me about something when she accidentally knocked over one of the tubes that she was taking to the lab. I had this feeling, and yes, I was right. The chlamydia tube had fallen to the floor, smashing into a million pieces. I had to take off my pants and underwear and open my legs and get that speculum back in to redo the test for chlamydia! It turns out that I did not have chlamydia. After all the trauma!

Fox F, 15

151

Some infections can be transmitted sexually AND also in ways that have nothing to do with sex. Check out these too (and also trichomoniasis earlier in this chapter).

Urinary Tract Infection (UTI)

What is it and how do you get it?

It is an infection of your bladder (the sac that holds your pee), and your urethra (the tube that your pee travels through). UTIs are often caused by a bacteria from your bowels. UTIs happen when the bacteria travels to your urethra during intercourse, oral sex, or when you wipe yourself with toilet paper from the back to the front. You can get UTIs from factors that have nothing to do with sex.

How do you know if you have it?

• You have to pee a lot, but only little bits at a time.
• It burns when you pee and there may be blood in your pee.
• Your pee smells bad or it is not clear.

What should you do?

Go to your doctor. They will be able to tell you if you have it by your symptoms and by testing your urine. They can give you antibiotics, which will help make the infection go away.

Yeast Infection

What is it and how do you get it?

Yeast is a fungus. It's not as gross as it sounds. It grows in our vaginas anyway, but if we have too much, it causes itching and soreness. These infections are very common. They are really irritating, but they aren't life threatening.

Yeast infections are caused by an overproduction of yeast. You can get one without having sex, but it can sometimes be transferred between genitals during sex. That means that if you have sex with a guy while you have an untreated yeast infection, he can get itching and redness on his penis and have discomfort.

You can get yeast infections from:
• eating too much sugar
• taking antibiotics
• taking the birth control Pill
• sexual partner who has a yeast infection
• wearing restrictive clothing that doesn't let your vagina breathe
  or synthetic underpants
• too much stress
• drinking and smoking can also make it worse

How do you know if you have it?
• itching, redness, and swelling of the vagina
• discharge that is thick and white, like cottage cheese
• pain when you have sex

What should you do?

A doctor can tell if you have one from the discharge and a swab. Yeast infections often come and go on their own. If they don't go away, you can get medicine from the drug store or from your doctor. Acidophilus pills from the drug store can be inserted in the vagina overnight. Alternatively, putting yogurt that contains acidophilus culture in your vagina can help treat the infection or take away some of the pain and discomfort. The easiest way to do this is to dip a tampon into plain yogurt and then insert the tampon into your vagina overnight. Try it three or four nights in a row. It may also help to allow your vagina time to breathe by wearing cotton underwear and loose clothing.

The Pap Smear Breakdown

Pap smear: a test to detect cervical cancer

Heads up, ladies, I've got a secret … Pap smears aren't that bad! Honestly … it's not painful, it's awkward … like having your arm bent in a weird way or something. The worst part of going to get a Pap is not knowing what to expect! So here's a quick heads-up:

Pap smears are strongly suggested for girls who are 18+ and/or sexually active. Before the actual test, you'll probably want to pee. It makes things a bit more comfy. Next, the doctor is going to ask you about your sexual activity, medical history, and all that doctor-type jazz. Remember, it's confidential, so be honest! Seriously, this is important. If you leave out facts or don't tell the whole truth, the doctor won't have a full picture of what's going on—it can screw things up. Having sex within 24 hours of the Pap can cause inaccuracies.

The doctor will tell you to undress and you'll lie on your back with your knees bent and legs apart on a table. Your feet might be put into stirrups. You'll feel pressure as the lubricated speculum is inserted … brace yourself, it might be cold! The speculum is holding your vagina open so the doctor can take a look-see and take the swab. If you're not comfortable with the size of the speculum, you can request a smaller one. The swab will be used to test for cervical changes.

If you're having a full pelvic exam, the doctor will also take different swabs to test for STIs. The speculum is then removed and TA-DA. You're done. It only takes a minute, literally.

Pap smears can be uncomfortable, but it's important to get them yearly for early detection of cervical cancer. I know it's weird to have your legs spread on a table in a doctor's office, but keep in mind, doctors do this alllll the time; it's normal. They won't be weirded out or turned on by your vagina; it's just a medical procedure to your doctor. If you're still uncomfortable, try finding a female family doctor, or going to a sexual health clinic, which is much more anonymous.

Imogen Birchard

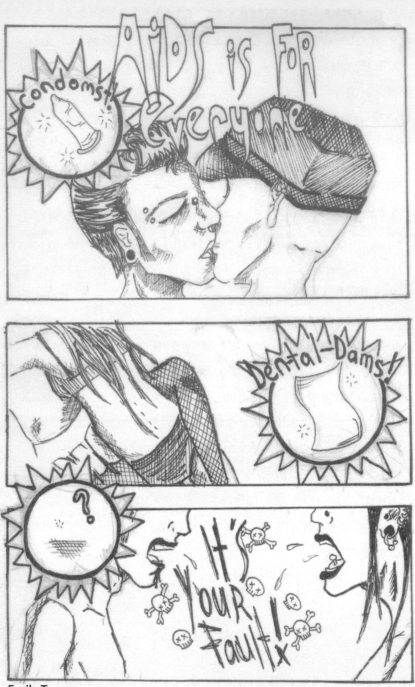

Emily T.

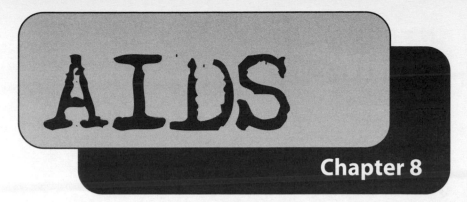

AIDS

Chapter 8

AIDS ... it's such a scary word. I worry that we are forgetting about AIDS and how serious it is. People all over North America are still contracting HIV. This makes sex so scary.

AIDS is something we all have to learn about and it's something we need to really think about before we have sex. Yes, it's a drag but so is DYING. In this chapter, there are personal stories and a lot of facts that can help you to understand how to take care of yourself. Hey, grrrls, let's stop messin' around and look out for ourselves! Read on to find out how.

Chi Nguyen

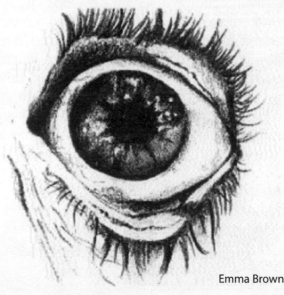

Emma Brown

Questions We Had About
HIV/AIDS
and Answers We Found
Reseached and Written by the Group

Q. What does HIV mean?

A. HIV stands for human immunodeficiency virus. It is a virus that works really slowly to destroy your immune system. This breakdown of the immune system is called AIDS (acquired immune deficiency syndrome). So AIDS is a later stage of HIV infection.

Q. What does it mean if you have HIV?

A. If you have HIV antibodies in your blood it means you are infected with HIV. A positive test does not mean you have AIDS. It does mean that you can pass the virus onto others through blood, vaginal fluids, semen, and breast milk.

If the HIV infection worsens, it develops into AIDS; your immune system breaks down and you may get very sick from infections and could die from an AIDS-related illness. If you are HIV positive, it is time to start taking care of yourself. Start eating better, resting more, and protect yourself from other STIs. There are special treatments that can really help. Getting good medical attention is very important and so is emotional support. See the resources at the back of this book for a list of organizations that can provide you with information and support.

Q. What is AIDS?

A. It stands for acquired immune deficiency syndrome. It means your immune system has been weakened by HIV so your body cannot fight off illness. There is no cure for AIDS, but medications keep improving.

Q. What does it mean if you have AIDS?

A. AIDS is a medical diagnosis that means that HIV has weakened your immune system to the point that your health is threatened. You are at risk for serious opportunistic infections—in other words, infections that take advantage of your low defences.

Q. How can you get HIV? I thought only older people who have anal sex or use drugs get it.

A. People used to think it was a "gay" disease but that is not true. A lot of young men and women are HIV positive.

There are three things that must exist for someone to pass HIV from one person to another:

1. One person must have the virus present in their blood, semen, vaginal fluids, or breast milk.
2. There must be a sufficient amount of the virus in the body fluid that's passed to the other person. Blood, semen, and vaginal and cervical secretions can carry a lot of the virus. Other body fluids like sweat, tears, and saliva don't carry enough of the virus.
3. The virus must penetrate through the skin and into the body. This can happen through a number of ways: vaginal sex, anal sex, and sharing needles and sex toys are high risk. Fisting, rimming, and oral sex are low risk activities that can transmit the virus. The virus can be passed from mother to infant in the uterus, labor, or through breast-feeding. If you have another STI, it makes it easier to be infected with HIV.

Q. Can lesbians get AIDS?

A. There is a myth that lesbians cannot get AIDS. First off, a lot of lesbians have sex or have had sex with men, and there are lesbians who use needles. HIV can be found in vaginal fluids and blood, including your period blood. If you have oral sex with a woman, you could get HIV through the small sores or small cuts in your mouth as well as through fingering or sharing sex toys. If a women already has an STI or is on her period, the risk will be increased.

Q. If you are HIV positive, will you have AIDS?
A. If you are HIV positive, the virus will not necessarily develop into AIDS in the near future. It can take up to 15 years before you show symptoms of AIDS. But the virus will still be multiplying in your body.

Q. How can you find out if you have HIV?
A. You can get tested. There are a few ways you can do this:
• First (and most common) are blood tests. These include the **standard blood test** and the **rapid blood test**. The standard blood test tests antibodies from blood samples and gives results within 2-3 weeks. In the US, you can get a rapid blood test, which gives results in less than an hour.
• Second, there is the **oral mucosal transudate test**. This test checks for HIV antibodies in oral fluids (but not saliva) by placing a special pad in the mouth, between the lower cheek and gums.
• Third, there is the **urine antibody test**, which tests for antibodies in – you guessed it – your pee.
Check with your local clinics to find out what kind of testing they do in your area.

Q. Are the tests confidential?
A. There are different types of testing systems, but all are confidential.
Voluntary (or Nominal) Testing: Most doctors and hospitals use this system, in which the test results can be traced to you. This means your name is on the test. In the US, only hospital or clinic personnel and state health departments can access your files. You have to sign a written permission form before your information can be revealed to others.
Anonymous Testing: Under this system, the hospital or clinic doesn't take your name so there is *no* way they can trace the test result to you. You make the appointment by phone. In the US, you are assigned a random number to link you with your test. In Canada, you can use your first name or a code. Your address and phone number are not needed. After 2-3 weeks, you return to the clinic to get the results. In Canada, results are not given over the

phone. In the US, anonymous testing is only available in 39 states. Check with your local clinic to see if anonymous testing is available in your area.

Q. Can you get HIV the first time you have sex?
A. Yes, definitely! You can get HIV the first time you have sex. Always protect yourself.

Q. Are there teenages who have HIV?
A. Yes, there are lots! According to a 2004 UNAIDS report on the global AIDS epidemic, young people aged 15–24 account for half of all new HIV infections worldwide. There are a lot of issues for youth that are HIV positive. Many of them become homeless, because families kick them out. Some of them are using drugs and this affects their ability to maintain good health. Many young people don't know they are infected. Young women should also be aware that if they are HIV positive and pregnant, they can take medication that lowers the risk of their baby being infected. You may want to talk to your doctor about getting an HIV test if you are pregnant. (See resource guide at the back for more info.)

Suvi Siu

A Young Woman Who is HIV Positive

Jasmine is 17. She lives in her new apartment in Toronto. She has a temporary job at Voices of Positive Women. She is attempting to attend university. She is HIV positive.

Jasmine grew up in Ottawa, with parents she describes as narrow-minded. In her eyes, her mother's duty was to be a perfect housewife, while her father brought home the money. She was taught to believe she wouldn't be good enough, that she was stupid and inferior. Her brother, with the lower marks at school, was always praised and commended for his excellent work. Her parents had told her she was a mistake, the result of a bad acid trip.

During her childhood, Jasmine had a blood transfusion. She needed the transfusion after an operation.

Around her birthday, turning 12, Jasmine started experimenting with drugs. She first tried marijuana, acid, and hash. Then she used cocaine and heroin. Jasmine started sharing needles and abusing these substances. It was through the blood transfusion or the drug use that Jasmine contracted HIV.

When she was 15, Jasmine went in for a HIV test. She was nervous and alone. When the results returned, they were positive. Jasmine told her mother that afternoon, and was booted out of the house for good. She hitchhiked to Toronto, where she lived on the streets for about 6 months. Jasmine realized it was time to get her life back into shape. She went to Evergreen, an organization dedicated to helping street youth. They helped direct her to other organizations, and from there she was guided to Voices of Positive Women.

Over the past 2 years, Jasmine's life has been turned upside down. Through the organizations like Evergreen and Covenant House, she has managed to regain control of her life. Yet, it's still difficult for her to balance the pressures of her life. Jasmine does a lot of speaking to schools and community agencies about HIV and AIDS. She spends a lot of time doing this kind of work as a way to cope with her disease. Jasmine enjoys educating her peers about the virus. She believes that the key to stopping prejudice against AIDS patients is education. Jasmine hopes that through her speaking and educating, she can help dispel the myths and prejudices against people with HIV or AIDS.

Chi Nguyen

The Down Low: What You Should Know

Corrine Aberdeen

This piece is just the tip of a massive iceberg.
These are the basic facts about the "Down Low,"

because what you don't know could hurt you

Definition:
- slang phrase implying secret information, but also used to describe black subculture of "straight" men having sex with men

The Facts:
- Men on the "down low" engage in sex acts with other men while continuing sexual and romantic relationships with women.
- Men on the "down low" don't consider themselves gay or bisexual; the same-sex sexual behavior is usually only for physical pleasure.
- Men on the "down low" don't identify as gay, due to the stigma attached to being gay in the black community; in general, the image portrayed of a gay man is a stereotypically flamboyant and effeminate white man.

Effect on Women:
- Because of the secretive nature of this male-to-male sex, it is unlikely that the contraction of STIs (especially HIV/AIDS) would be disclosed by a man on the "down low" to a female partner.
- Health officials believe that men on the "down low" may be a health risk to their wives and girlfriends.

**So the moral is, ladies, knowledge is power!
The more you know the safer you are.**

What Is Safe Sex?

Safe sex means a lot of things; there is emotionally safe sex and physically safe sex. I am going to focus on physically safe sex.

The safest thing to do is not to have sex. But the reality is that we often choose to have sex and most of the time we don't know what the risks are. When I first had sex, I was worried about getting pregnant but I didn't really think it would happen to me and I didn't think about STIs or AIDS. Once I learned about these things and met young people who were my age and HIV positive, I changed my mind about sex. Now I insist on safe sex.

I have done a lot of reading and learning while working on this book, and to have the safest sex possible is the ideal, but I wonder how many people actually do have the safest sex they can? I think we should begin by talking about what safe sex is:

To ensure safer sex with a penis in a vagina, you need the following:

- latex or polyurethane condom with spermicidal gel, cream, or foam
  OR a polyurethane female condom
- water-based lubrication (Oil-based lubes can cause condoms to break.)

165

To "go down on a woman," you need the following:

- dental dam or a latex condom cut in half (A dental dam is a soft thin stretchy piece of latex that feels silky. You hold it between your partner's vagina and your tongue while giving her oral sex. It feels really good and also helps prevent the spread of STIs.)

To give a blow job to a guy, you need the following:

- a dry latex condom

To finger a woman, you need the following:

- latex gloves or finger cots

So there you have it,
your safest bet is LATEX CONDOMS!!!!! (But remember: even condoms aren't 100% effective—it says so right on the package.)

Now that you know you need to use condoms and all the other goodies, does that mean you will?

Why don't some people use condoms?

I have heard so many guys say "it doesn't feel good" or "I'm too big, it doesn't fit properly" or "It ruins the mood".
So how can we respond to these statements? Here is a list of suggestions of what to say.

- "It may not feel good, but having a little swab stuck up inside your penis for an STI check feels even worse, don't ya think?"

- "It may not feel great, but green discharge coming out of your penis is not a such a good feeling either!"

- "I can see that you're big, but as you can see I can fit this entire condom on my fist so I think it will fit!" (Try it. You really can!)

- **"Not to worry, I have the extra large condoms. Let's see if you really need them."**

- "Yeah, you know what? Testing positive for HIV would ruin MY mood."

- "You know what ruins my mood? The fact that you don't care about my safety! And you say you love me!"

- "I understand that it could ruin the mood BUT if I put it on with my mouth like this, how does it feel?" (Try this one too.)

- **There is this saying "no glove no love..." That works for me!**

Another thing we have to keep in mind about condoms is that a lot of guys don't actually know how to put them on. If that thing is going in my body, I want to know the condom is on the right way!!! See the following picture for instructions.

A lot of friends say that they won't put them on a guy because they don't want him to think they are sluts. Well here is some news for you. If he thinks those types of things, then why are you about to sleep with him? I always put the condoms on and I make it a part of the foreplay. That way the so-called mood isn't ruined.

In the end, what did we learn? USE CONDOMS TO SAVE YOUR BODY, RELATIONSHIPS, and LIFE!

Emily T.

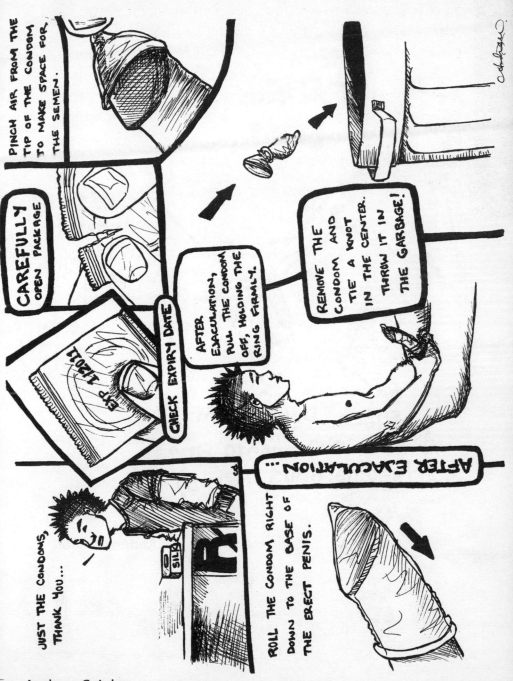

Andrew Coinbra

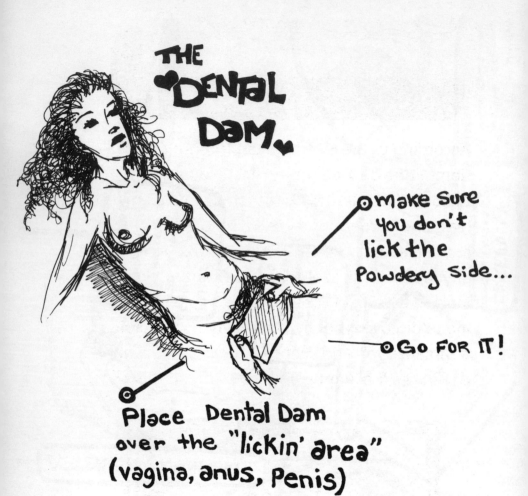

Andrew Coinbra

Sexual Assault

Chapter 9

According to the Metropolitan Toronto Action Committee on Violence Against Women and Children (METRAC), 51% of women experience at least one incident of sexual or physical violence in their lifetime. Sexual assault can happen to anyone at any time. And it's never the victim's fault. At a point in your life when you're just starting to discover your own sexuality, it can totally traumatize you and change your life. This chapter deals with the intense emotions around this issue.

Chi Nguyen

That Night

I died that night you stole from me, and now I'm here

I'm in some place my pain is real

I don't know what to do

I feel that coldness of your hard hands

I feel me shaking, crying, lying in your shame

I did nothing wrong except going with you

I said nothing but NO

I remember that night, I'm now scarred for life

I still feel you and my stomach gets weak

I feel horrible and you made me crazy

Get out of my head, leave me alone

I died that night you stole from me

I said nothing but NO.

Anonymous, 17

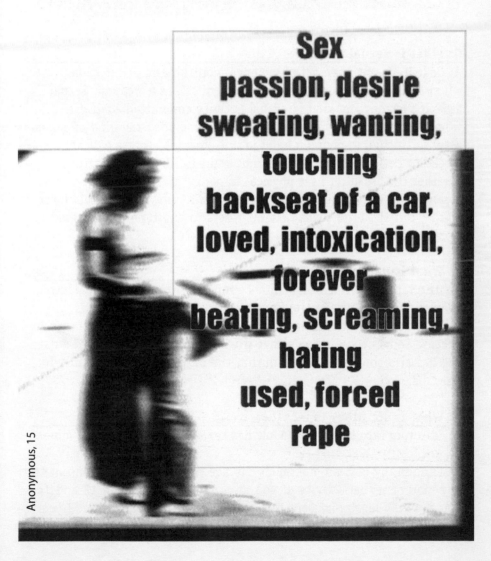

Sex
passion, desire
sweating, wanting,
touching
backseat of a car,
loved, intoxication,
forever
beating, screaming,
hating
used, forced
rape

Anonymous, 15

Questions We Had about
Sexual Assault

Answers provided by Bridget Sinclair,
Youth Services Worker, St. Stephen's Community House

Q: What is sexual assault?

A: Sexual assault is an act of violence, control, and domination, when an individual uses the act or idea of sex as a weapon. Sexual assault includes any kind of sexual activity committed against a woman when she does not want it. It also includes any kind of sexual activity (including giving a hand job or blow job) that a woman is forced to perform when she does not want to. It doesn't matter whether the assaulter uses physical force or threats, it is still sexual assault. The word rape is often used to define unwanted sexual intercourse, but the term sexual assault refers to any type of unwanted sexual activity.

Q: What is date rape?

A: Date rape, also called acquaintance rape, is sexual assault committed against you by someone you know and trust. This person ends up betraying your trust. Dealing with date rape can be especially difficult because some people assume that if a woman has consented to a date she has also consented to sex during the date, and this is definitely not true.

Q: What is statutory rape?

A: Statutory rape is when an adult has sexual intercourse with a minor.

In Canada, by law, no one under the age of 12 can legally consent to any kind of sexual activity. If you are between the ages of 12 and 14, you can only legally consent to sex if your partner is less than 2 years older than you. It is illegal for anyone over the age of 18 to have sex with anyone under the age of 18 if there is more than a 2 year difference in their ages. It is also illegal for someone in a position of authority (like a teacher or a coach) to have sex with someone younger than 18. Be careful if any of this applies to your relationship; the law doesn't consider the way you feel about someone regardless of age, and just because you believe "age ain't nothing but a number" doesn't mean the courts will agree. Canada's legal system now uses the term sexual interference instead of statutory rape.

In the United States, the age of consent differs from state to state, but nowhere is it lower than age 16. According to federal law, it is illegal for a person to have sexual intercourse with anyone under the age of 16 if there is more than a 4 year difference in their ages.

Q: What factors affect a woman's risk of being sexually assaulted?
A: Women of any age can be assaulted, but there are some adverse social conditions that can put a woman at a higher risk of experiencing sexual assault. A lack of housing, being a runaway, and/or being financially desperate are all factors that can make a woman more vulnerable to sexual assault.

These factors appeal to perpetrators of sexual assault who often look for people they can easily take advantage of, people they feel more powerful than, and people who won't report the assault to police or other authorities. For the same reasons, perpetrators of sexual assault tend to prey on people with low self-esteem. A person with low self-esteem may find it difficult to stand up for themselves and to say what they want (or don't want), and they may even feel like they don't deserve to be treated well. Nobody deserves to be sexually assaulted.

Q: Is it important for women to report sexual assault?
A: It is important to report sexual assault to the police so that the attacker doesn't get away with it and assault other people. Unfortunately, many women have mixed feelings about going to the police. Some women fear that the process of charging someone will make an already horrible experience even more difficult to deal with.

Other women are afraid the police officers they talk to will be very insensitive.

Fortunately, many police departments have officers who are specially trained to help women who have been sexually assaulted. They will gather evidence and help the woman get medical treatment and counseling. The police, not the woman, will lay the charge against the assailant; the woman will be a witness. Whether or not a woman decides to report a sexual assault, it is important she makes the decision herself.

If you are sexually assaulted, whether or not you decide to tell the police, it is very important to get medical treatment as soon as possible, either at a hospital emergency room or a clinic. You should go even if you feel okay physically because you may have injuries you don't know about yet. If your assailant had any STIs, a doctor or nurse can offer treatment (such as prophylactic antibiotics) immediately. They can also evaluate your risk of getting pregnant from the assault and offer options including the emergency contraceptive pill. They can also offer you counseling and support. If you are under a certain age, usually 16, the hospital or clinic may be required by law to report your sexual assault to the police and to a child protection agency.

You can also call a sexual assault hotline if you are unsure what to do. See the back of this book for information on how to find numbers in your area.

Q: If you are sexually assaulted, what is the first thing you should do?

A: There are a number of different ways to deal with and work through being sexually violated. You may or may not decide to involve the police. Either way, it's essential that you take care of yourself at this time.

Here are some ways to take care of yourself immediately after being sexually assaulted:
- Leave the area where the sexual assault happened and go somewhere you feel safe and comfortable.
- Call someone you trust and feel comfortable with. This could be a close friend, a parent, a social worker, or any other trustworthy adult.

176

- Remember that you are not to blame. Whatever the situation was, the assault was not your fault.
- Be sure to spend the next few days with someone you trust. Do not stay by yourself, because this will be a very difficult time.

You may also wish to do the following things if you are thinking about involving the police:
- Go to a hospital emergency room or clinic, where social workers and doctors will give you support, connect you to other support services in your area, and examine you.
- Call someone you trust and feel comfortable with who can come and be with you for support.
- Before you go for medical treatment, you should not have a shower or a bath. It may be difficult to not clean yourself because you might feel dirty, but it is important that you don't. There may be evidence on your body from your assaulter that can be collected and used against him in court.
- You should write down everything about the sexual assault, including where and when it happened, who assaulted you (if you know), and what exactly happened.

Q: How do you know you just haven't misinterpreted someone's actions?

A: Your body and past experiences will tell you when something is wrong. Remember, sex is not something you owe someone, nor is it something that you should be forced into.

Q: Is it rape if your spouse or partner forces you to have intercourse?

A: Definitely. Rape is an act of violence, control, and domination that some spouses will try to use against their partners. It is not your wifely duty to have sex with your spouse. You decide when you want to have sex. If you did not consent and your partner has intercourse with you, then it was rape. It doesn't matter if you've consented on previous occasions or even if you are married; if you don't consent to sexual activity and it happens anyway, it is sexual assault.

Q: Which is more common: being attacked by a stranger or by someone you know?

A: Women are more often sexually assaulted by someone they know than by a stranger.

Q: If you don't feel safe with someone, what should you do?

A: Follow your intuition. If you don't feel all right, get away. Go somewhere safe. Talk to someone supportive. Try to always have bus or cab fare with you so you can get home on your own; always have a plan on how you are getting home.

Q: Do only men commit sexual assault?

A: Sexual assault is not gender specific, but men assaulting women is the most common form of sexual assault. Men also sexually assault other men, women sexually assault women, and sometimes women sexually assault men.

Q: Can you become pregnant from a sexual assault?

A: Yes, it is possible. But a woman can go to a clinic and get the emergency contraceptive pill as soon as possible – it is effective up to 72 hours after sex.

Q: Should women be more aware of rapes and date rapes on college and university campuses?

A: A number of factors put women at a potentially higher risk of sexual assault on a campus. There is this idea around college and university that everyone wants to party and that getting sex is an important part of the whole experience. There is also a lot of drinking and a lot of substance abuse on campus that can impair judgment. Campuses also have publicly accessible areas that are often isolated and/or poorly lit.

Colleges and universities take the issue of sexual assault very seriously. To improve safety, most campuses have implemented programs such as security escorts for students, improved lighting in isolated areas, and floor supervisors in residence. It's important to remember that, no matter where you live, you are at risk and you need to take precautions to protect yourself.

Q: Is it still rape, even if you didn't say no, but still felt you were forced into it?

A: Yes, it is still rape if things like coercion and threats were used. It is rape if you were not free emotionally, physically, and/or mentally to say no.

Q: What is the best way to say no to someone?

A: The best way to say no is loud and clear – NO!! You don't have to explain or justify why. It is important that you are demanding and firm with your response to the person that you are with. In these moments you can't be shy or worry about offending the person. Protect yourself. Taking a self-defense course may help you develop confidence in dealing with this kind of situation.

Q: Is there anything a woman can do about men who make cat calls at her when she walks down the street?

A: These men are looking for a reaction, so the best thing to do is to ignore them.

Q: If you wear revealing clothes, are you asking for an assault?

A: No, not at all. A woman's dress, hair, and manner are not an invitation to violate her. Men can and should control themselves just as women do.

Q: Is it true that a man who violates a woman can't control his sexual desires?

A: No! Many men who commit sexual assault already have a sexual partner. It is not usually due to "lack of sex" that drives them to assault women. Men are responsible for their acts of violence! Women have the same urges as men do, and therefore, men can control themselves just as women can. Again, rape is not about sexual desire, it is about power and control.

See the resources section at the back of this book for how to find more information on sexual assault.

WAYS WOMEN CAN PROTECT THEMSELVES

Buddy Systems—When you are out at night, stay with a friend and make a deal to look out for each other. If you are drinking, look out for each other. In clubs, keep an eye on your friend and check in with each other.

If you are with a partner, be as clear as you can about what you want sexually and what you don't want—and let him know.

If a man makes sexist comments or jokes, or doesn't respect what you want or say, then you may not want to be around that person anymore. If you have no choice but to be around him (if he is a teacher of yours or something), try not to be alone with him, and let other people know that that man makes you uncomfortable.

Avoid isolated places—When you're walking alone day or night avoid alleys or areas where there are no other people. Always be aware of who is around you and what they are doing. If you can, always carry enough money for a cab or bus.

Beware of Rohypnol™ and other date-rape drugs—These are drugs that some men are putting in women's drinks in clubs and bars. What has been happening is that a guy will try to pick up a young woman. He will slip the pill in her drink. Soon she will start to feel sleepy and ill. He will then offer to take her home and eventually she will pass out. Then he will sexually assault her. Watch your drink. Don't take drinks or drugs from a stranger. Date-rape drugs have no taste and are odorless, so you can't tell if any is in your drink. If you lose time or memory, are nauseous or vomiting, and feel like something happened "down there", consider getting medically checked out. You may have been sexually assaulted.

WENDO—WENDO is self-defense for women only. There are many types of self-defense and many are offered through community centers.

What is sexual harassment?

Sexual harassment can be a number of things, including the ones listed below.
• staring or leering at someone
• pinching a person
• patting a person
• repeated sexual comments
• pressuring someone for a date
• grabbing someone
• using body and strength to intimidate someone

Any of the actions listed above are considered sexual harassment if they are UNWANTED by the woman. Sexual harassment can happen in any situation. Sometimes it occurs when a man has power over a woman. Examples of this include a teacher who has power over a student, an employer who has power over an employee, a parent who has power over their child, or a group of men who have power over one or two women.

All my life, I have been told that it's a
BIG
BAD
world
out there.

Get a man to walk you home at night, or you'll get kidnapped and raped. My curfew is adjusted depending on my relationship status: if I've got a boyfriend to walk me home, I can stay out as late as I want; if I'm single, it's home by midnight. The fear of nighttime and isolated areas has been embedded in me. Never once was I warned that a friend, a boyfriend, a teacher could sexually assault me—only bad men lurking in dark, scary alleyways. The truth is that a boyfriend, husband, acquaintance, or relative commits most of the rapes. Even though I know that and have even experienced the reality first-hand, I am still most scared of those dark isolated nights walking home—not of parties, school dances, or my boyfriend's house. Because I want to believe that this shit only happens in dark, scary alleyways. Not in my own home, with someone I trust.

Imogen Birchard

I didn't know what to do; I felt I had to just go with it. I guess I should have screamed or maybe even ran. I was afraid and so many things were running through my mind. I can't believe this happened because it has changed so much. I think about it now and it hurt.

I knew this guy. He has lived in my area for a long time. I went with him because I guess I kind of trusted him. I thought that he would respect me, or even stand up for me. I was wrong.

He started with a touch and ended with a scar. I should have done something but my **NO** should have been enough.

I GUESS ONE DAY

Anonymous, 16

I guess one day maybe
I will get over this
I hope each day and until then my pain is real
I can't erase the past
I'm working on the future
I know what happened to me
You will not make me weak
I'm beautiful and smart
You once made me ugly
I hate how you treated me and now you will pay
I don't know what I'll do but
I hope your conscience might help
Tell me how does it feel to just take and not care?
Tell me how do you walk and keep your head high
Are you proud of yourself?

Jessica Johnston

184

8 RED BULL BEERS

Love beat into me that night
it fisted me
and made me cry
I pretended that I liked it
So maybe he'd like me
and I lay there
My legs spread
My thighs hot and bruised
I couldn't bare to live after this war was over
(I prayed he would kill me)
And I was already dead when he hurt me
and raped me
and I told him I loved him.

FOX F, 15

185

Untitled

Robbed of her innocence
Fiction its place
She thought when she grew older
Memories would loose their sour taste.

He ran off with her security
Leaving wounds that never heal
Took away her purity
Which she now longs to feel.

And as she lays in darkness
Upon shame-ridden sheets
She dreams of a time
When her screams will come to cease.

As the tears wet her cheeks
A heart cries out in pain
Her vulnerable self is helpless
A prisoner that can't escape.

A blanket of hate caresses
Her eyes filled with rage
She sits and digs
Her own dark, sullen grave.

And who is here to help her
Push away her poisoned mind
Undo the coils that bind
To let her inside shine.

Anonymous, 16

Devoured innocence

In a moment all the petals on a rose can fall down on a cold bitter floor
And in a moment, innocence can be devoured
along with spirit and so much more
In a moment your whole world can change
And anything in that moment is out of control, out of your range
remember YOU are not the one to blame, so feel no shame

To whom this may concern, child I feel your agony, and I also bleed your pain
There is no reason to feel scared, dirty, or ashamed.
Don't be afraid to cry, weep when no one's there, although it sounds absurd
Because, baby, believe, all of your silent tears are heard
All your thoughts have been thought and all your feelings have been felt,
you're not alone
You think everything will be alright once you insert that clip in your dome
You think that will make the pain go?
NO
Survive for the many it will happen to
Once you grow to learn how, you can help turn their silent tears into laughter
No matter who is reading this, remember the world needs your smile
… once again you're never alone, but don't worry you'll eventually learn this
even if it takes a little while
so although your innocence has been devoured
know that those mother fuckers did it because they're LOW
and they feel the need to be empowered
think about it, what a FUCKING SLIMEY LITTLE COWARD
RISE ABOVE, don't be frightened because your spirit still shines through
although you don't know me, know I BELIEVE IN YOU
your petals have not fallen, you're still a unique work of art
and to all the tainted angels, I have a place for you in my heart
so this goes out to all the spirits that have tried to be broken
i'm speaking for the beautiful innocent people
who remain unheard and unspoken
and who think suicide is the token
I HEAR YOU, I FEEL YOU, AND I BLEED YOUR PAIN
so please listen when I say, I promise, I promise, I promise
that one day …
Everything will be okay …

Kasha Arthuton Cheung

Emma Brown

Little Black Book for Girlz Resource Guide

We hope you find the following numbers and websites helpful. However, they are not meant to replace professional advice. Their inclusion does not constitute an endorsement by the authors or the publisher. Please also keep in mind that phone numbers and website addresses and content are subject to change.

Kids Help Phone – **www.kidshelpphone.ca** – 1-800-668-6868 (CANADA)

Kids' Helpline – **www.kidscrisis.com** – 1-877-KIDS-400 (UNITED STATES)

CHAPTER 1: RELATIONSHIPS
Healthy Relationships:
Advocates for Youth – **www.advocatesforyouth.org**
Go Ask Alice! – **www.goaskalice.columbia.edu**
Teenwire.com – **www.teenwire.com**
Youth Embassy – **www.youthembassy.com**
Youthwork – **www.youthwork.com/youthinfo.html**

Lesbian, Gay, Bisexual, Transgender, Transexual, Two-Spirited, Intersex, Queer and Questioning Relationships:
The National Coalition for Gay, Lesbian, Bisexual & Transgender Youth – **www.outproud.org**
PFLAG (Parents, Families and Friends of Lesbians and Gays) – **www.pflag.org**
PFLAG Canada – **www.pflagCanada.ca**
Youth Resource – **www.youthresource.com** (Health/Sexuality/Relationships – for LGBTQ youth)

Transgender Info:
Transproud – **www.transproud.com**
Youth Resource – **www.youthresource.com/living/trans.htm**

Homophobia/Transphobia/Biphobia/Heterosexism:
Advocates for Youth – **www.advocatesforyouth.org/lessonplans/activistally1.htm** (Fighting Homophobia and Transphobia)
Bi Resource – **www.biresource.org/pamphlets/biphobia.html** (Fighting Biphobia)
Canadian Rainbow Health Coalition – **www.rainbowhealth.ca/english/homophobia.html** (Challenging Homophobia/Heterosexism)
Gay-Straight Alliance Network – **www.gsanetwork.org/resources/straight.html** (Straight Allies)
Trans Accessibility Project – **www.queensu.ca/humanrights/tap/3discrimination.htm** (Fighting Transphobia and Discrimination)

Emotional/Mental Abuse:
National Youth Violence Prevention Resource Center www.safeyouth.org/scripts/teens/dating.asp (Teen Dating Violence) 1-866-SAFEYOUTH (1-866-723-3968) (US and Canada)
Love Is Not Abuse – www.loveisnotabuse.com
Teen Relationships – www.teenrelationships.org

CHAPTER 2: PERIODS
General Info:
Being Girl www.beinggirl.com (site by Tampax and Always)
Museum of Menstruation – www.mum.org
The Red Spot – www.onewoman.com/redspot (Periods – info, history, culture, questions answered)

Alternative Menstrual Products:
www.keeper.com , www.divacup.com , www.lunapads.com , www.gladrags.com, www.natracare.com /products/feminine_products.htm, www.seventhgeneration.com/our_products/women.php

CHAPTER 3: SEX
General:
Afraid to Ask – www.afraidtoask.com
BirdsAndBees.org – www.birdsandbees.org
Canadian Federation for Sexual Health/Planned Parenthood Federation of Canada – www.ppfc.ca
Canadian Health Network – www.canadian-health-network.ca – Select language and then click on link to Youth for relationships and sexual health
The Coalition for Positive Sexuality – www.positive.org
The Coalition for Positive Sexuality: Just Say Yes Campaign – www.positive.org/JustSayYes
Feminist Women's Health Center – www.fwhc.org/teens/index.htm
Guttmacher Institute – www.guttmacher.org (Abortion/Sex/Relationships/STIs/Pregnancy)
It's Your (Sex) Life – www.mtv.com/thinkmtv/features/sexual_health/iysl_guide/index1.jhtml
Options for Sexual Health (OPT) – www.optionsforsexualhealth.org
Planned Parenthood Federation of America, Inc. – www.plannedparenthood.org
Scarleteen: Sex Education for the Real World – www.scarleteen.com (Heath/Sexuality/Relationships)
Sex, Etc.: By teens for teens – www.sxetc.org (Health/Sexuality/Relationships)
Sexual Addiction Hotline – 1-800-310-3001 (US only)
Sexuality and U – www.sexualityandu.ca
Sexuality Education Resource Centre Manitoba Youth Site – www.serc.mb.ca/SERC/YO/WA
Society for Human Sexuality – www.sexuality.org
Spider Bytes: A New Spin on Sexual Health for Teens – www.spiderbytes.ca
Teens Health – www.kidshealth.org/teen/ (Health/Sexuality/Relationships)
Toronto, City of, Public Health/Sexual Health – www.toronto.ca/health/sexualhealth/index.htm

LGBTQ:
Gay, Lesbian, Bisexual & Transgender National Youth Talkline -1-800-246-7743 (US only)
www.glnh.org
Lesbian Gay Bi Trans Youth Line – www.youthline.ca
National Gay & Lesbian Hotline – 1-888-843-4564 (US only)
National Youth Advocacy Coalition – (Les/Bi/Gay Youth) – www.nyacyouth.org

People with Disabilities:
Baylor College of Medicine – Centre for Research on Women with Disabilities –
www.bcm.edu/crowd/?PMID=1332
BC Coalition of People with Disabilities www.bccpd.bc.ca/s/Sexuality Disability asp
Canadian Federation for Sexual Health – www.ppfc.ca/ppfc/content.asp?articleid=409 (Sexuality
and Youth with Physical Disabilities)
Disability Cool – Women's Stuff – www.geocities.com/HotSprings/7319/woman.htm
Queers on Wheels – www.queersonwheels.com (LGBTQ with Physical Disabilities)

People of Color:
Ambiente Joven – www.ambientejoven.org (Sexuality resource for LGBTQ youth in Spanish)
GINE Web – www.unizar.es/gine/hola.htm (Spanish health site)
My Sistahs – www.mysistahs.org (Sexuality resources for young women of color)
National Latina Institute for Reproductive Health – www.latinainstitute.org
National Black Women's Health Imperative – www.blackwomenshealth.org
Advocates for Youth: Info and Support for Youth of Color – www.advocatesforyouth.org
/youth/info/yoc.htm

Age of Consent:
Legal Age of Consent – www.ageofconsent.com/ageofconsent.htm
Avert – www.avert.org/aofconsent.htm

CHAPTER 4: BIRTH CONTROL
General Info:
The Association of Reproductive Health Professionals (ARHP) – www.arhp.org/patienteducation
/interactivetools/choosing/index.cfm?ID=275 (Interactive quiz to find method of birth control right
for you)
Girl's Guide to Condoms – www.managingdesire.org/girl'sguidetocondoms.html
Lea's Shield – www.leasshield.com/index.htm
Health Canada – www.hc-sc.gc.ca/hl-vs/sex/control/index_e.html

Emergency Contraception:
Back Up Your Birth Control with Emergency Contraception – www.backupyourbirthcontrol.org
The Emergency Contraception Website – www.NOT-2-LATE.com
Ann Rose's Ultimate Birth Control – www.ultimatebirthcontrol.com

CHAPTER 5: PREGNANCY/MISCARRIAGE
Teen Pregnancy:
American Pregnancy Association – **www.americanpregnancy.org**
National Advocates for Pregnant Women **www.advocatesforpregnantwomen.org**
StorkNet – **www.storknet.com**
TeenParents.org – **www.teenparents.org**
Girl.Mom (support, community, and education for young mamas) – **www.girlmom.com**
Motherisk – **www.motherisk.org/women/index.jsp** (Substance abuse and medical conditions
during pregnancy) 1-877-327-4636 – Alcohol and Substance; 1-888-246-5840 – HIV and
HIV Treatment

Miscarriage:
Richmond Health Services – **www.rhss.bc.ca/bins/content_page.asp?cid=101-196-529** (Physical
and emotional reaction to miscarriage)
Robyn's Nest: The Parenting Network – **www.robynsnest.com/Books/miscarriage.htm**

CHAPTER 6: ABORTION
General Info:
Abortion Clinics On-line – **www.gynpages.com** (US and International Clinics)
Abortion Hotline – 1-800-772-9100 (both Canada and US)
After Abortion – **www.afterabortion.com** (Post Abortion Syndrome)
Birth Mother.com – **www.birthmother.com** (for women who are considering placing a child for
adoption (pre-placement), and those who have placed (post-placement))
Choice USA – **www.choiceusa.org** (Pro-Choice)
Exhale – **www.4exhale.org** (after-abortion counseling helpline – 1-866-439–4253 – English,
Spanish, Cantonese, and Vietnamese-speaking counselors available)
Feminist Women's Health Center – **www.fwhc.org/abortion**
Indigenous Women's Reproductive Rights and Pro-Choice Page – **www.nativeshop.org
/pro-choice.html**
NARAL – National Abortion and Reproductive Rights Action League – **www.naral.org**
(Pro-Choice)
National Abortion Federation – **www.prochoice.org** Hotline – 1-800-772-9100 (US only)
1-800-424-2280 (Canada only)

Statistics:
Guttmacher Institute – **www.guttmacher.org/sections/adolescents** (Statistics about many topics
including abortion) (USA)
Statistics Canada – **www.statcan.ca** (CAN)

CHAPTER 7: STIs
American Social Health Association – **www.iwannaknow.org**
Health Canada – **www.hc-sc.gc.ca/dc-ma/sti-its/index_e.html**
LesbianSTD – **depts.washington.edu/wswstd**

CHAPTER 8: AIDS
HIV/AIDS:
AIDS Committee of Toronto – **www.actoronto.org**
AIDS and Sexual Health Hotline – **1-800-668-2437, 1-416-392-2437** (Canada)
Asian Community AIDS Services – **www.acas.org**
Avert – **www.avert.org**
The Body – **www.thebody.com** (extensive AIDS/HIV site)
Canadian Aboriginal AIDS Network – **www.caan.ca**
Centers for Disease Control and Prevention – **www.cdc.gov/hiv**
Health Canada – **www.hc-sc.gc.ca/dc-ma/aids-sida/index_e.html**
Know HIV/AIDS – **www.knowhivaids.org** – **1-866-344-KNOW** (US only)
Motherisk – **www.motherisk.org/women/hiv.jsp** (HIV treatment in pregnancy)

National AIDS Hotline (US only)
1-800-232-4636
1-800-344-7432 Español
1-888-232-6348 Deaf Access (TTY)

National Minority AIDS Council – **www.nmac.org**
The National Native American AIDS Prevention Center (NNAAPC) – **www.nnaapc.org**
National STD/AIDS Hotline – **800-342-2437** (800-342-AIDS) (US only)
TeenAIDS – **www.teenaids.org**

Safer Sex:
Public Health Agency of Canada – **www.phac-aspc.gc.ca/publicat/epiu-aepi/std-mts/condom_e.html**
AIDS Committee Toronto – **www.actoronto.org/website/home.nsf/pages/mysexlife**

CHAPTER 9: SEXUAL ASSAULT
Sexual Assault:
Feminist Majority Foundation – **www.feminist.org/911/assaultlinks.html**
GirlsHealth.Gov – **www.girlshealth.gov/safety/relationships.htm**
The Network Against Abuse in Same-Sex Relationships – **www.bcifv.org/resources/samesex.shtml**
Network/LARED Ending Abuse in Lesbian, Bisexual Women, & Transgender Communities
– **www.thenetworklared.org**
RAINN (Rape Abuse & Incest National Network) – **1-800-656-HOPE** (US only) **www.rainn.org**
Sexual Assault Care Centre – **www.sacc.ca**

Sexual Harassment:
New York City Alliance Against Sexual Assault – www.nycagainstrape.org/survivors_factsheet_60.html
Surviving to Thriving: Healing and Hope for Survivors of Sexual Violence – www.surviving tothriving.org/factsandmyths

Self-Defense:
Rape Aggression Defense Systems – www.rad-systems.com
Wen-do – Women's Self-Defense – www.wendo.ca

Other Cool Links:
Aboriginal Youth Network – www.ayn.ca
AdiosBarbie.com – www.adiosbarbie.com (Body Image)
Canadian Youth for Choice – www.cfsh.ca/youth (Policy-Making)
The Deaf Queer Resource Center (DQRC) – www.deafqueer.org
National Organization for Women – www.now.org (Activism)
Project Respect – www.yesmeansyes.com
Radiance Magazine – www.radiancemagazine.com/issues/1999/spring99_teen_scene.htm (Body image and size discrimination)
Spank Mag! Youth Culture Defined by Youth – www.spankmag.com (forums related to sexuality and relationships)
Youth Action Network – www.youthactionnetwork.org (Youth Activism)

Glossary

abortion – When a woman decides to end her pregnancy and has an operation to remove the embryo or fetus from her uterus

abstinence – To abstain from sex – meaning to not have sex

AIDS – Acquired Immune Deficiency Syndrome: a medical condition caused by HIV that destroys the body's immune system and leads to death

anal sex – Just like it sounds: inserting something (penis, dildo, finger…) in the bum hole for pleasure

anus – Bum hole

bisexual – A person who is physically and emotionally attracted to both men and women

blow job – Slang for oral sex on a guy: using the mouth on the penis for pleasure

cervix – The narrow lower part of the uterus that has an opening that connects the uterus to the vagina

clitoris – The female sex organ that is located between the labia at the upper end of the vulva; stimulation of it can make a girl have an orgasm

condom – A thin small baggy that is made of latex or polyurethane and that covers the penis to catch all ejaculate fluid

contraceptive – Something that helps prevents pregnancy

cum (come) – Slang for ejaculation and/or semen; also slang for orgasm (male or female)

cunnilingus – The clinical word for oral sex on a girl; using the mouth/tongue on a women's vagina for pleasure

cyber sex – When people use the internet to talk to others in an arousing or sexy manner

cyst – A fluid-filled mass or bump growing on or inside the body that is usually sore but not serious or harmful

date rape – Rape or sexual assault by someone a woman is on a date with or is seeing, dating, etc.

date rape drug – A drug that can be slipped into a woman's drink, making her unable to function properly or take care of herself (even pass out), allowing the person who slipped the drug to take advantage of the woman sexually

dental dam – A thin piece of material that is silky and soft, to hold over the vagina during oral sex to stop fluid exchange

diaphragm – A shallow, dome-shaped cup a woman places inside her vagina against the cervix to help prevent pregnancy by preventing sperm from reaching the egg

dick – Slang for penis

dildo – A rubber toy, usually shaped like a penis, that is used for sex

discharge – A slighty thick fluid from the vagina, usually onto underwear

doggy style – Slang for a sexual position where one person is on their hands and knees and the other person penetrates from behind

douche / douching – Using scented water to clean the vagina and cervix. Douching can encourage certain infections of the vagina. For most women, it is unnecessary because the vagina is a self-cleaning organ with its own secretions.

down low – Slang for a person in a heterosexual relationship but having sex with the same sex secretly

dyke – Slang for lesbian

eating out – Slang for oral sex on a girl

ejaculation – When a guy cums and his penis squirts semen

embryo – A fertilized human egg before it grows into a fetus (at about 8 to 12 weeks after the sperm fertilized the egg)

Fallopian tube – Inside a woman's body, one of two narrow tubes that carry an egg from the ovary to the uterus

fellatio – The clinical word for oral sex on a guy (blow job)

female condom – A polyurethane pouch worn by a woman during sex; it entirely lines the vagina and it helps to prevent pregnancy and STIs including HIV

fetus – An embryo after it has taken the rough shape of a human (at about 8 to 12 weeks after the sperm fertilized the egg)

finger cot – A device resembling a male condom and used to cover the fingers during sex; it helps protect against STIs

fingering – Slang for having intercourse with fingers in a partner's vagina rather than a penis

fisting – Inserting a fist in another person's anus or vagina for sexual stimulation

foreplay – All the stuff that gets you excited before sex: flirting, touching, rubbing, kissing, licking …

fuck buddy – Slang for a chosen friend who you have sex, but not a serious relationship, with

gay – Being physically and emotionally attracted to someone of the same sex

gender – The characteristics and behavior that society expects from a person based on that person's biological sex

go down – Slang meaning to give oral sex

G-spot – A small area on the front wall of the vagina that is especially sensitive to sexual stimulation in some women and may be the source of a small amount of fluid ejaculated at orgasm

hand job – Slang for using your hand to rub a guy's penis until he cums

head (giving head) – Slang meaning to give oral sex

heterosexual – Being physically and emotionally attracted to someone of the opposite sex

HIV – Human immunodeficiency virus: the virus that causes AIDS. It can be passed from an infected person through blood, semen (cum), vaginal fluids, or breast milk. Activities like unprotected sex and sharing needles are at a high risk for transmitting HIV.

ho – Slang for whore or slut

homosexual – Being physically and emotionally attracted to someone of the same sex

hormones – Natural chemicals in your body that affect how your mind and body work. Women tend to have more estrogen hormone, and men tend to have more testosterone.

hymen – A thin piece of tissue that stretches across part of the opening of the vagina. It is usually broken by first-time sexual intercourse but can also break from bike riding, horseback riding, or other activities.

labia – The lips of the vagina

lesbian – A woman who is emotionally and physically attracted to other women

lube / lubricant – A water-based slippery substance used in sex to make things more comfortable and safe. Oil-based lubricants can damage condoms and so should not be used.

masturbation – Touching oneself in a sexual manner for pleasure with fingers, toys (such as dildos), etc.

menstruation – A woman's period: the time of month that her uterus sheds its lining, and the blood and tissue comes out her vagina. When a woman is pregnant, she does not have her period: the lining stays in the uterus to protect the egg.

Menstrual cup – A small soft plastic cup to place inside the vagina to catch menstrual blood (used instead of tampons)

miscarriage – When a pregnant woman's embryo or fetus unexpectedly leaves the uterus before it can survive on its own; also known as a spontaneous abortion

oral sex – Using your mouth and tongue on your partner's genitals to excite him or her

orgasm – The feeling, during sex or masturbation, of the greatest pleasure and release of pressure from your muscles contracting. With guys, this usually happens when he ejaculates.

ovary – The organ inside a woman's body that releases an egg once per month

ovulation – The point in a women's cycle where her body produces an egg and it is released from the ovary into the Fallopian tubes. An egg fertilized with sperm results in pregnancy.

ovum – The egg that women's bodies releases once per month from the ovary

pad – A piece of material a girl uses during her period to absorb the menstrual blood; also called a maxi-pad, sanitary pad, or sanitary napkin

Pap smear – A test to detect cervical cancer. Your doctor wipes a bit of tissue from your cervix and looks at it under a microscope.

penis – The male sex organ

period – When a women menstruates, meaning the blood and tissue from her uterus come out through her vagina. This is usually once per month and lasts a few days.

phone sex – Simulating sex by describing it to someone on the phone

Pill (the Pill) – Short for birth control pill; a pill taken daily to prevent pregnancy

queer – Slang for being of a different sexuality than straight (heterosexual)

rag (on the rag) – Slang for getting your period (menstruating)

rape – Unwanted sexual intercourse

rimming – Performing oral sex on someone's anus

semen – The white stuff that comes out of a guy's penis when he ejaculates. It contains sperm, the male sex cells that combine with a woman's egg to make her pregnant.

sex toy – Any object that is designed and used to make sex fun and exciting

sexual assault – When someone is forced into any sexual act or has any sexual act forced upon them against their will

shag – Slang for sexual intercourse, having sex

sixty-nine – Slang for a sexual position where both partners are able to give oral sex to each other at the same time

slut – A slang word that is meant to demean women for having a lot of sex or for having sex with someone besides their steady boyfriend or girlfriend

speculum – A small plastic or metal device placed in a woman's vagina to help a doctor examine inside

sperm – The male reproductive cell that combines with a woman's egg to make her pregnant. When a guy ejaculates semen, it contains many, many sperm.

spermicide – A gel that contains a chemical that kills sperm before it can fertilize a woman's egg

spotting – When a girl's menstrual blood comes out a little bit at a time instead of as full period

statutory rape – A legal term to describe when an adult has sex with someone who is not old enough to consent to sex according to the law. In Canada, this term has been replaced with the phrase "sexual interference."

STD – sexually transmitted disease; also called sexually transmitted infection (STI)

STI – sexually transmitted infection; also called sexually transmitted disease (STD)

straight – Slang for heterosexual

tampon – A small cylinder of cotton (or a similar material) that is placed up into the vagina to absorb menstrual blood.

transgendered – When a person feels that the gender they were assigned at birth does not reflect the gender they feel inside themselves

uterus – The pear-shaped organ in a woman's body that holds and nourishes a fertilized egg as it grows from embryo to fetus to a baby ready for birth. The narrow lower part of the uterus becomes the cervix, a canal that connects to the vagina.

vagina – A woman's internal genitals: the tunnel that begins between the legs of a woman and leads inside her body to the cervix and uterus

vaginal sex – Penetration in the vagina for sexual gratification by fingers, penis, toys, etc.

virgin – Someone who has never had sex before

vulva – A woman's external genitals, including the labia, the clitoris, and the opening to the vagina

womb – The area of your body where a baby grows; same as uterus

yeast infection – An overproduction of yeast in the vagina, which causes pain and itching

About St. Stephen's Community House and the Drug-Free Youth Arcade program

St. Stephen's Community House is a unique, community-based social service agency that has been serving the needs of Kensington Market and surrounding neighborhoods in downtown West Toronto since 1962. Operating with a staff of over 150 people and with the support of almost 400 volunteers, we provide services for more than 32,000 people a year. St. Stephen's addresses the most pressing issues in its community – poverty, hunger, homelessness, unemployment, isolation, conflict and violence, AIDS, racism, youth alienation, and the integration of refugees and immigrants.

Specifically, we will endeavor to maintain and to enhance our role as a leader and partner in the community by providing:
• A quick response to community needs
• Access to a range of services for children, youth, adults, and seniors
• Immigrant and refugee support programs
• Advocacy to improve the quality of life of our community
• Support for community capacity building
• Effective, high impact programs

ARCADE'S MISSION: To provide a range of youth services that (1) meet emerging and critical youth social, health, recreation, and education needs; (2) empower youth to speak, advocate, and lead youth programming that impact on their lives; (3) assist youth facing a range of barriers and life experiences through the transition to young adulthood safely and confidently; (4) To encourage youth to think critically about themselves and the community in which they live.

How do we make sense of our mission? The Arcade has become the hub of the youth community in our neighborhoods. Youth know it to be a place where they can get information in a non-judgmental and supportive environment. Parents know it's a safe place where their kids can hang out and socialize with their peers while getting information and support. In addition, the Arcade programs are designed to assist youth make the transition from being a teenager to a young adult. Programs support our youth educational endeavors, support their social skills and learning, develop their leadership skills, and build resilience. Funders know it as a well-managed, youth driven program with strong community networks. St. Stephen's Community House and the Youth Arcade receive on-going financial support from the City of Toronto and the United Way of Greater Toronto.

www.ststephenshouse.com

Acknowledgments

First of all we would like to thank all the young women who pushed their personal boundaries and dug deep to write honestly and openly about their experiences, ideas, and feelings, and committed their time to make this book happen.

The original writers: Suvi Siu, Emma Brown, Annie Grainger, Chi Nguyen, Chauntae Walls, Hilary Quigley, Kristina Pelletier, Rebecca Hodgson-Dewitt. You have no idea how great what you started has become: you have reached so many people's minds and hearts.

The revisers: Imogen Birchard, Corrine Aberdeen, Emily Trinh for taking over the early stages of revisions. Your flare was essential to putting forward a great book.

Outreach: Cyesha Ford and Azia Negru-Harsman who were responsible for getting this valuable information to those young women living in rural Ontario.

We would like to thank Jessica Harrod and Kate Scowen for listening to the concerns of the young women in the Youth Arcade, seeing the potential, and finding resources to make the project happen.

A big thanks to The City of Toronto Public Health who helped fund this project and supported it throughout the years of development by providing valuable information and expertise.

Throughout the process of research and writing this book we had tremendous support from community professionals who gave their time and effort to ensure that this book was factually correct without losing the voices of the young women who wrote it. All the professionals who assisted us in the process were chosen because of their unique approach with youth, their open-mindedness, and their ability to keep information accessible and engaging.

A big thank-you to all the young women who hang out in the Youth Arcade who voiced their opinions, their experience, and their criticism in order to have the material in this book be applicable to diverse youth cultures.

A big thanks to David Wichman, who corresponded with us almost daily for months to get this book into publishing form. Thanks for your patience!

A large thanks to all the Youth Arcade staff at St. Stephen's Community House over the last few years who supported and hyped up this book to everyone everywhere, and for being so intensely committed to our youth community and the issues youth face.

Last but not least, a sincere thank-you to St. Stephen's Community House (Liane Regendanz, Bill Sinclair, and our dedicated Board of Directors), for their consistent innovation, their commitment to young people, and their courage to take risks within programming in order to best serve the members of our community.

Bridget Sinclair, *Youth Community Worker*
Marlon Merraro, *Manager, Youth Services*
St. Stephen's Community House

Annick Press Acknowledgments

Annick Press would like to thank the following individuals for reviewing the manuscript and offering their professional input:

Kym Halliday, *RN, CCRN, SANE-A (Sexual Assault Nurse Examiner), New Mexico*

Karen Leslie, *Karen Leslie, MD, FRCPC, Staff Paediatrician, Division of Adolescent Medicine, Associate Professor of Paediatrics, The Hospital for Sick Children and The University of Toronto*

Sally O'Neill, *RN, M.Sc. Director of Healthy Body Talk*

Index